the 50 BEST
SCIENCE &
TECHNOLOGY
STOCKS
for CANADIANS

2002 edition

the 50 BEST SCIENCE & TECHNOLOGY STOCKS for CANADIANS

2002 edition

Marco den Ouden

MACMILLAN CANADA
TORONTO

First published in Canada in 2001 by
Macmillan Canada, an imprint of CDG Books Canada

Copyright © Marco den Ouden 2001

Canadian Cataloguing in Publication Data

Den Ouden, Marco
   The 50 Best science and technology stocks for Canadians

2002 ed.
Previously publ. under title: The 50 best Internet stocks for Canadians / Mark Pavan, Gene Walden and Tom Shaughnessy.
Includes index.
ISBN 0-55335-015-4

1. Stocks 2. Internet industry — Finance. I. Pavan, Mark 50 best Internet stocks for Canadians. III. Title. IV. Title: Fifty best science and technology stocks for Canadians.
HD9696.8.C32D36 2001   332.63'22   C2001-901593-3

This book is available at special discounts for bulk purchases by your group or organization for sales promotions, premiums, fundraising, and seminars. For details, contact: CDG Books Canada Inc., 99 Yorkville Avenue, Suite 400, Toronto, ON M5R 3K5. Tel: 416-963-8830. Toll Free: 1-877-963-8830. Fax: 416-923-4821. Web site: cdgbooks.com.

1 2 3 4 5 WC 05 05 03 02 01

Cover & text design: Kyle Gell Design

Macmillan Canada
An imprint of CDG Books Canada Inc.
Toronto

Printed in Canada

CONTENTS

Editor's Note   *vii*

Acknowledgements   *ix*

Introduction   **1**

Biology, Medicine, and Environment   **37**

Biovail Corporation   38

Patheon Inc.   42

Axcan Pharma Inc.   46

Forest Laboratories, Inc.   50

Pfizer Inc.   54

ArthroCare Corporation   58

MDS Inc.   62

Merck & Company, Inc.   66

Canadian Medical Laboratories, Ltd.   70

Zenon Environmental Inc.   74

Energy   **79**

Calpine Corporation   80

Pason Systems Inc.   84

Canadian Hydro Developers, Inc.   88

Trican Well Service Ltd.   92

Industry   **97**

Cree, Inc.   98

ATS Automation Tooling Systems Inc.   102

Magna International Inc.   106

Bombardier Inc.   110

Gennum Corporation   114

Silent Witness Enterprises Ltd.   118

BW Technologies Ltd.   122

DuPont Canada Inc.   126

CAE Inc.   130

Tesma International Inc.   134

Magellan Aerospace Corporation 138

Information Technology **143**
AOL Time Warner Inc. 144
CGI Group Inc. 148
Check Point Software Technologies Ltd. 152
EMC Corporation 156
Mercury Interactive Corporation 160
Microsoft Corporation 164
Network Appliance, Inc. 168
Siebel Systems, Inc. 172
Solectron Corporation 176
Yahoo! Inc. 180
Intel Corporation 184
Cognos Inc. 188
THQ Inc. 192
Sapient Corporation 196
ATI Technologies Inc. 200
Celestica Inc. 204
Internet Security Systems, Inc. 208
The Thomson Corporation 212

Telecommunications **217**
Aastra Technologies Ltd. 218
C-MAC Industries Inc. 222
Comverse Technology Inc. 226
PMC-Sierra, Inc. 230
Research in Motion Ltd. 234
Wescam Inc. 238
BCE Inc. 242

Glossary *246*
The 50 Best Stocks in Alphabetical Order *249*
Index *251*

EDITOR'S NOTE

No book, website, or expert can ever truthfully guarantee what will happen to a given stock. The best any of them can do is provide information and a context for that information to help the investor make the best choices for him or her. I think with the 2002 edition of The 50 Best Series, we have provided more information, and a reliable context by which to understand it. Through our partnership with the Canadian Shareowners Association, The 50 Best Series provides up to 10 years of financial history, where available. Almost everyone else provides only five years of data.

We assembled an Advisory Board, consisting of Rob Carrick, Ellen Roseman, and Mary Cordeiro, to give advice on how to improve the series and to help us draft screens and measures that our authors could use in selecting the "50 Best" for each book. The Advisory Board gave us lots of specific and helpful ideas, many of which have been incorporated into the books and which I believe have improved the series. Their energy, wit, and thoughtfulness were deeply appreciated.

The authors themselves cheerfully took on the task of working within the boundaries set by our Advisory Board and researched extensively the companies that would meet all these requirements and give investors a reliable and interesting selection to consider in building a portfolio.

It's my hope that with the benefit of this winning combination of data, selection criteria, and research, you will have the means to create a portfolio that helps you outperform and prosper.

Good luck!

Joel Gladstone
Editor

ACKNOWLEDGEMENTS

Writing a book is no easy task, though I certainly thought it would be when I started the project. But it was a most enjoyable experience all the same. I learned a lot about a lot of companies and I hope I've succeeded in imparting some insight into the "50 Best" firms, their histories, their products, and their prospects in the text.

Thanks to Patrick McKeough, publisher of *The Successful Investor*, and Peter Winter of *Canadian Biotech News* for suggestions on stocks to include. Thanks also to Ryan Irvine and Brent Larsen of *The FutureStock Review* for an interesting discussion and their insights. Valuable ideas were also garnered from several other newsletters: *Bob Czechin's Oil & Energy Report*, *The Cabot Market Letter*, and *Addicted to Profits*. The Canadian Shareowners Association's Stock Guide software proved extremely useful in analyzing historical data. And the Center for Research in Security Prices at the University of Chicago supplied some hard-to-get information.

I'd be remiss if I didn't mention two large influences—the writings of William O'Neil of *Investor's Business Daily* in his book *How to Make Money in Stocks*, and Donald Cassidy of Lipper Financial Services in his book *It's When You Sell That Counts*.

My wife, Janis Baker, and children, Adriaan and Sarah, were very supportive while I banged away at the keyboard, Jan often bringing me cups of fresh tea to keep me going.

Finally I'd like to thank Joel Gladstone, finance editor at Macmillan Canada, for giving me this wonderful opportunity and his constant encouragement and support. And of course, the editor of this book,

Sarah M. Wight, who knows her Strunk and White. She cleaned up my excessive verbiage, rearranged things where it improved coherence, and suggested useful changes. Rebecca Conolly did a super job of coordinating the final production of the book.

My biggest debt is to Joe Internet for the wonderful invention that bears his name (or to whoever really invented the Internet!) Most of my research was carried out on the Net, and without it, this book would not have seen the light of day.

The book's virtues were improved by the influence of all the above. Any deficiencies, of course, are of my own making.

Happy reading!

Marco den Ouden

INTRODUCTION

Why Science and Technology? Why Now?

"It was the best of times, it was the worst of times, it was the age of wisdom, it was the age of foolishness, it was the epoch of belief, it was the epoch of incredulity, it was the season of Light, it was the season of Darkness, it was the spring of hope, it was the winter of despair…"

— Charles Dickens, *A Tale of Two Cities*

Dickens was writing about the years leading up to and including the French Revolution, but this marvellous turn of phrase could easily be applied to the last few years in the stock market.

The best of times—September 1998 through March 2000—was the era of dot-com millionaires (some would say dot-com madness) and the NASDAQ soaring to 5000—a period of optimism and hope. In workplaces across the country the chatter reached a fever pitch in the early months of 2000. "Hey, I made five grand on my stocks yesterday"; "You want a hot tip? Take a look at XYZ.com"; "What do you think of ABC.com?"; "My barber says LMNOP.com is a winner"; "At this rate I can retire in five years, maybe sooner"; "We're all going to be stinking rich!"

That was January and February. Then March came in like the proverbial lion, but didn't go out like a lamb—more like a dog slinking away with its tail between its legs. The NASDAQ gained 5 percent in the first 10 days of March, closing at 5049 before it sputtered and collapsed—dropping below 4500 by month's end and barely missing 3000 when it bottomed on May 23, 2000. A 40 percent drop.

Next came the summer rally. We'd seen the best of times and the worst of times—now was the time for belief: We're in this for the long haul, and the market will come back. After all, hadn't the market bounced back in '98 after a few months? And bounce back it did, with a vengeance, hitting 4275 on July 17, 2000, for a 42.5 percent gain.

A minor correction followed before the index again climbed back, but the NASDAQ only made it to 4250 before it was time for incredulity, the season of Darkness, and the winter of despair! Like Icarus after flying too close to the sun, the NASDAQ plunged down, down, down to bottom out at 1620 on April 4, 2001. A drop of 61.9 percent from September 2000 and 67.9 percent from its March 2000 peak.

I mention the NASDAQ, of course, because it is widely regarded as the bellwether of science and technology stocks. Whither goes the NASDAQ, there go the techs. I do not mention the crash to scare the bejeebers out of you, though it should give you pause to reflect.

Is It Over Yet?

But is the bear market in science and technology stocks really over? Some hard money enthusiasts and value investors believe that valuations are still too high. David Skarica, the bright young writer of *Addicted to Profits*, argues in his May 2001 issue that bull markets never begin immediately after the burst of a speculative bubble (and the NASDAQ crash was the burst of a speculative bubble). Rather, he thinks the market will enter a long-term trading range of five, 10, or even 20 years before another bull starts. There will be rallies, mini-bulls, if you will, within this period, followed by mini-busts, but his long-term projection is a flat or underperforming market in technology stocks. Mr. Skarica cites Sir John Templeton, the legendary value investor: The run-up in the tech market was "the biggest financial insanity ever in any nation in history," and we could be in for "maybe a nine-year bear market."

Patrick McKeough, Canada's ace stock-picker, two-time winner of the *Globe and Mail*'s "One and Only" contest (including 2000 with his pick of CAE, also one of the 50 Best), doesn't quite see it that way. He predicted the bull market of the 1990s in his book *Riding the Bull*, and has further predicted that the bull market will not end in a conventional bear market but will evolve into a two-tier market with selected stocks rising while the rest are flat or declining. To some extent, we have already seen this. When the IT, Internet, and telecom sectors were booming, many other stocks were underperforming. Mr. McKeough was referring to the overall market, not just technology. More significant for our subject is his prediction that the composition of the tiers will shift. And today we have seen a shift away from the high flyers of 1999 and early 2000 and into the energy sector, banking and finance, retailing, and value plays. In fact, some analysts are saying the next "bubble" will be in today's value stocks. Mr. McKeough predicts the next hot sector will be biotechnology. He sees the shifting of sectors into and out of favour as all the more reason to have a diversified and balanced portfolio.

All the prime ingredients of the bull market are still there: trade liberalization, productivity gains from technology, and the maturing of the baby boomers. To these "economic energizers," as he calls them, he's added tax reduction. The long-term health of the market, says Mr. McKeough, will not be adversely affected until we see a revival of inflation and an inversion of the yield curve (when long-term interest rates are lower than short-term rates).

On May 19, 2001, the *National Post* sported the screaming headline "Inflation Hits Nine-Year High." Gold prices appear to have hit bottom around the same time. The U.S. Federal Reserve has been pumping up the money supply at unprecedented rates. But long-term bond yields have been going up, not down, while short-term rates have declined under Alan Greenspan's aggressive rate cutting in the first half of 2001. So we have a return of inflation, but no inverted yield curve. It remains to be seen where price inflation will head in the near to mid-term. Much of the price inflation is related to high energy costs, which are a market and not an inflationary phenomenon.

Does this mean we should play it safe and keep out of the stock market? Actually, quite the opposite! Today we are facing unprecedented opportunity. The NASDAQ crash was a necessary purge of speculative excess from the marketplace. It is part of the price of progress. But the Internet, the communications revolution, new advances in medical science, progress in miniaturization and nanotechnology, strides in materials science—all of these are happening now and will continue into the future. They still offer opportunities for investors to prosper.

The Power of Innovation

Science and technology, in fact, offer some of the best opportunities for investors in the marketplace. The reason is the power of innovation. The sole distributor of a product or service commands a distinct market advantage and a unique profit opportunity. Many science and technology companies are on the cutting edge of development—innovating and bringing new products to market. Being first with a product, particularly one protected by patents, gives a company a quasi-monopoly position in the market.

Sometimes this advantage translates into long-term market dominance that makes the company a giant among its fellows. Consider Intel Corporation. In 1971 Intel developed the microprocessor, the key building block of every personal computer. Its first application was in a calculator developed by the Japanese company Busicom. A few years later, the fourth generation of microprocessor, the famous 8086–8088 line, went into IBM's new personal computer.

What did this mean for investors? Quite simply, it created many a millionaire. Someone lucky enough or smart enough to have invested US$10,000 when the company went public in 1972 would have netted US$5,610,106 on April 4, 2001, at the bottom of the NASDAQ crash. At Intel's peak she would have pulled down a cool $18,752,014.

But what if she had missed Intel in 1972, or even when IBM came out with the PC in 1978? By early October 1987, Intel stock had risen 31-fold from its launch price. Then came the crash, and Intel plunged from US$62.75 to a low of US$27.00, a 57 percent drop in three weeks. An investor at that point could have thought, "Well, I guess this one's peaked. Too late to get in now." Or she could have seen it as an opportunity: Intel on sale! If she had plunked down US$10,000 at that point, she could have made over US$1,344,444 at the August 2000 peak. Sold on April 4, 2001, she would still have netted US$402,222.

Many technology stocks are at a similar point today. They are on sale. Some have risen three-fold or five-fold or eight-fold and will be going up even more. Still others will sputter and fail.

You might think that investing in science and technology stocks is not for the faint of heart. It might be more accurate to say it's not for the faint of brain. Investing in science and technology stocks—indeed, investing in any stock—is an active process requiring thought and consideration. You can't just invest in a tech stock and leave your money there (though that would have worked with Intel, Microsoft, and many others). You have to think about what you're doing. That thinking comes in three distinct phases:

1. Think about what you're going to buy.
2. Having bought, think about whether you should continue to hold the stock.
3. As circumstances change, think about when to sell.

The middle phase—thinking about holding—might seem odd to many. But as Donald Cassidy, a senior analyst with Lipper, puts it in his classic book, *It's When You Sell That Counts*, holding a stock should be an active and not a passive decision. Later in this introduction I'll discuss how to select a science and technology stock and when to consider selling it. But first—what exactly is a science and technology stock?

What Is a Science and Technology Stock?

Through the latter half of 2000 and the first quarter of 2001, newspaper headlines were rife with references to the tech wreck, the collapse of the Internet bubble, and the failure of technology stocks. The implication was that technology meant the Internet, computers, and the infrastructure supporting them.

But at a very basic level, almost any company is involved with science and technology. Take, for example, Acme Doorstop, a fictional company that makes nothing but doorstops. A doorstop is an inclined plane, one of the simple machines of high school physics. Its coefficient of friction is crucial—you don't want the doorstop to slip—so Acme's products put a scientific principle into action. Or consider Canada Bread, a real company. Baking bread involves a variety of chemical reactions, the knowledge of the effect of heat on certain materials, and figuring out an optimal mix of flour, sugar, eggs, and yeast to get the desired results.

Yet companies making doorstops or bread are not considered science and technology companies. They are low tech. That is, the science they rely on in their business is not new or rapidly evolving. When we think of science and technology, we generally think of high tech.

What is high tech? Even there we run into problems. Almost anyone would call computer hardware and software companies high tech, but what about auto manufacturers? According to the Massachusetts Institute of Technology's prestigious *Technology Review* Patent Scorecard (www.technologyreview.com), DaimlerChrysler has 722 patents, far outstripping the number held by Compaq Computer (426) or Microsoft (357). Surely the number of patents held should be an indicator of a company's involvement in technology?

Or consider Trican Well Service, a fast-growing Canadian company specializing in services to the oil industry. Its website (www.trican.ca) says that "Trican has grown into a full service supplier of state-of-the-art technology and expertise in coiled tubing, well fracturing, stimulation, cementing and related services." The oil industry is a complex one, involving geology, chemistry, engineering, and fluid dynamics. Companies servicing the oil industry are in fact involved in science and technology.

Then there are companies that are sometimes thought of as science and technology companies but that really aren't. The most famous of these is Amazon.com, one of the first companies to exploit the Internet in a big way. Internet companies are usually considered to be a branch of high tech, but isn't Amazon.com really just a glorified bookstore? Does it make money from the Internet? No. It makes money from selling books. (Or, more accurately, it loses money selling books.) The Internet is just the vehicle connecting it to its customers.

In fact, much of the Internet sector doesn't qualify, in this writer's view, as science and technology. All the companies that supply goods and services available in the bricks-and-mortar economy are really nothing more than stepped-up versions of the original retail concept. And many have found that the supposed step up was really a step down. As Internet stock prices collapsed, many companies selling toys, or pet food, went belly up. Other businesses have translated well to the Internet economy—banking and brokerage services have flourished and will continue to grow, as will travel agencies and fare brokers. But a bank is a bank is a bank, even if it does its business online instead of in a local branch.

Internet companies that do qualify as science and technology stocks are Internet portals, search engines, Internet service providers, application service providers, web hosting services, website designers, and Internet-related software developers.

So we return to our question: What is a science and technology company?

Our Definition

Science and technology companies are companies that are developing new ways of doing things and advancing the state of knowledge. Usually they have a budget for research and development, and often they hold patents on technology they have developed. Science and technology companies are innovators discovering new scientific knowledge and inventing new products and techniques. They make a significant portion of their revenues by developing or exploiting science and technology.

That would also include companies that are technology-driven, such as broadcasting and electronic data and information systems, even if they do not engage directly in research and development. Broadcasting companies, for example, are part of the great communications revolution, and will be even more so as we move to a convergence of the old telecommunications industries and the new. BCE, with its acquisition of the CTV television network, is a prime example and is one of the 50 Best. Such companies promote the development of technology by being the customers for the inventors, innovators, and developers.

This definition also includes companies supplying other businesses with support services involving technological expertise. These companies must stay on the cutting edge or die. For example, I consider Patheon Inc., a supplier of pharmaceutical outsourcing services, to be a science and technology company, even though it does its manufacturing and research on a contract basis for other companies. Or consider CGI Group, a computer solutions integrator. The company doesn't actually do research and development, but has to keep up with all the latest technology in order to install and manage computer networks for its clients. I have included Patheon and CGI in the 50 Best.

Another exception to the general principle that a science and technology company should be involved in research and development is the energy industry. This is an industry in flux, and some electricity-generating companies are technology-driven, even if they bring in technology developed outside the company. Companies such as Calpine are revolutionizing the business, bringing modern, clean, natural-gas-fuelled plants online to replace the coal-burning dinosaurs that many utilities still use. Others, such as Canadian Hydro Developers, are exploring alternative sources of energy: geothermal, wind power, or recycled waste.

Of the 54 sub-indices of the Toronto Stock Exchange, three are clearly involved in science and technology: Technology Hardware, Technology Software, and Biotech/Pharmaceuticals. But I have also considered Industrial Products, Communications and Media, Fabricating and Engineering, Chemicals and Fertilizers, Oil and Gas Services, and Utilities. Some, but not all, of the companies in these indices are science and technology companies for our purposes.

In this book I have divided the stocks into broad categories as well, defining five sectors that cover specific areas of the science and technology economy. To some extent, these sectors are independent of one another, and spreading investments across the categories will minimize risk.

- **Biology, Medicine, and Environment**—including biotechnology, pharmaceuticals, research labs, technical medical services, and environmental remediation.
- **Energy**—including electricity generation, alternative energy, and energy industry support services, but not including oil or mining companies.
- **Industry**—including aircraft technology and maintenance, automotive engineering, and general industrial engineering, as well as chemicals, plastics, and materials science.
- **Information Technology**—including computer hardware, software, and Internet applications.
- **Telecommunications**—including infrastructure developers, equipment developers and manufacturers, telephony technology, Internet service providers, and broadcasting.

Selecting the 50 Best

Science and technology stocks come in many flavours and colours, as I've noted. What characteristics should we look for to find the real winners to invest in? It comes down to two things: growth and profits.

These two factors, while ultimately crucial, may not be necessary in the short run. In fact, a science and technology company in its early stages often runs at a loss as it grows and develops. Growth alone—plus hype and hope—is often enough to move the stock price of a startup upwards. And then there are companies heavily involved in research, particularly in the biotechnology field, who may not have revenues, let alone earnings, as they work on product development. They survive on their capital, or on return on invested capital, as research progresses. The share price of these companies may go up considerably just on the promise that their research will be successful and lucrative products will be available in the future. Such companies, while interesting, are too speculative to be included in this book.

The Fast 50

Setting aside startups developing their first product, a good first step in searching for a good science and technology stock is to find companies with rapidly growing revenues. One of the best places to find such firms is the Deloitte & Touche Fast 500 and Fast 50 lists.

The Fast 500 is a list of the 500 fastest-growing public and private technology companies in North America (until 2000, it covered the U.S. only) based on revenue growth over the last five years. To be considered, a company must have had minimum revenues of US$50,000 five years previously and US$1 million in the most recent year. The company must also be one that develops "proprietary technology that contributes to a significant portion of the company's operating revenues, manufactures a technology-related product, or devotes a high percentage of effort to research and development of technology." Deloitte & Touche introduced the program to Canada in 1998 with the Fast 55 for 1997 (the Canadian revenue minimums are $75,000 and $1 million, and the list was later reduced to 50). In 2000, 45 of the Canadian Fast 50 made the big list, comprising 9 percent of the total.

There are two caveats about the Fast 50 and Fast 500 lists. First, they list companies that are growing fast in terms of revenues, not earnings. In fact, many, if not most, of these companies are in an accelerated growth phase and are money losers. Second, the list is not exhaustive: companies must be nominated for the annual competition. That said, the Fast 50 is a very useful guide to stocks with the potential to make significant gains.

What's truly significant for the investor is the stock market performance of these companies. At September 30, 2000, once the third Canadian Fast 50 list had been announced, there were 30 publicly traded companies that had made the list in previous years and 10 new ones. The 30 stocks from previous years had made an average gain of 355.95 percent, even though nine had fallen. A $1,000 investment in each stock as it made the list or went public would have turned $30,000 into $136,785 in two short years. March 30, 2001, was pretty well near the bottom of the technology market at the time of this writing. By then only 13 of the 40 stocks were in positive territory, while 27 were down. But guess what? Even with that many losers, the strength of the winners was such that the 40 stocks on average were up 20.6 percent. Five had doubled in price, or better. And Janna Systems (now Siebel Systems) was still up over 1,000 percent from when it first made the Fast 50. On the negative side, five of the 30 from 1998 and 1999 never gained more than 20 percent at their peaks. At March 30, 2001, 19 were down 50 percent or more, 11 were down 75 percent or more, and two were down over 90 percent.

What lessons can be learned from observing the Fast 50? First, there is some element of risk involved in investing in stocks purely on the basis of revenue growth. In fact, two of the top 50 of 2000's North American Fast 500 went bankrupt in 2001. Second, making the list

multiple years—that is, having continued growth—correlates with success. Four of the five that were double-baggers at the market bottom
were on the list three years running, and the fifth made the list two
years in a row. But making the list every year is no guarantee. Three
such stocks were down substantially on March 30, one never advanced
more than 10 percent at any time, and another was up 766.7 percent
at one point, only to finish down 66.7 percent at the market's nadir.
(Yes—you need to have a selling strategy!) Third, even the best stocks
can retreat after a strong advance. While it's true that Janna/Siebel was
still up 1,000 percent on March 30, 2001, at one point it had been up
4,858 percent. It dropped 80.9 percent from its high to its low. Again,
this points to the need to have some sort of selling plan. (If you haven't
guessed by now, I'm not a fan of buy-and-hold come what may.)

Making the Grade

Although it doesn't always hold true in the short term, there is a long-
term correlation between earnings growth, revenue growth, and share
price growth. The minimum criteria for the stocks included in the 50
Best, as determined by the Advisory Board, reflect this correlation.

- Stocks listed on TSE, NYSE, or NASDAQ for at least three years
- Average 10-year share price growth more than 10 percent annually
- Average 10-year earnings per share growth more than 5 percent
  annually
- Average 10-year revenue growth more than 5 percent annually
- Not more than one negative return on invested capital in any one
  of the last 10 years

These are fairly stringent requirements, but many excellent science
and technology stocks have less than 10 years' track record. So I also
looked for companies with superior revenue, earnings, and share price
growth since going public.

Canadians are fortunate in that we have a large and powerful industrial giant next door—the United States. We're doubly fortunate in that investing in American stocks is a piece of cake: Just call up your broker. (Americans are not as fortunate the other way around—unless they are dual-listed, Canadian stocks are difficult for Americans to buy.) Because of the robustness of the American economy and the tremendous opportunities there, as well as the fact that many Canadians like to buy U.S. stocks, I've included 20 of them here. Some, like Calpine, are listed on the TSE. Some Canadian companies, like PMC-Sierra, are not available on Canadian exchanges. Go figure.

In any event, diversification into some American stocks is not only good exposure to a very strong economy, but also affords protection against a declining Canadian dollar. You'll note that many of the Canadian companies covered are international players as well, with revenues derived globally.

How I Chose the 50 Best

Here is how I set about finding the 50 Best companies. First I went through the top 500 stocks on the TSE looking for one-year returns on March 31, 2001, and April 30, 2001. These were stocks that had actually forged ahead and made gains during the NASDAQ bear market. I compiled the data using the excellent filtering tools at Globeinvestor.com (my favourite stock research website). These lists contained few technology stocks, and were heavily dominated instead by oil and gas, banking, consumer, and industrial stocks. In fact, only about 50 could be considered science and technology stocks, even with the fairly broad definition outlined above. I then looked through these 50 or so stocks to select the companies that had grown earnings and revenues as well as share price. These were the first stocks on my list.

Second, I went through all the publicly traded stocks on the Fast 50 lists, employing the same criteria. I also examined other industry lists: *Profit Magazine*'s Profit 100, *Alberta Venture Magazine*'s 30

Fastest Growing Companies in Alberta, the T-Net British Columbia list of the 100 largest technology companies by revenue in B.C., and the Branham 300 list of the top information technology companies in Canada.

Then I looked at stocks on the following sub-indices of the Toronto Stock Exchange: Biotech/Pharmaceuticals, Technology Software, Technology Hardware, Industrial Products, Chemicals and Fertilizers, Fabricating and Engineering, Communications and Media, Utilities, and Oil and Gas Services. Enough stocks on these sub-indices qualified as science and technology in my book to warrant scouring through them.

Next I went searching for American stocks that qualified. The North American Fast 500 was just too big a list to go through, so I restricted myself to the top 50. I found *Fortune*'s September 2000 list of the 100 fastest-growing companies and an article called "Ten Stocks: The Best of the Bunch" (September 4, 2000). Nearly all of those stocks met the selection qualifications. The May 2001 edition of *Business 2.0* had an article called "Ten Tech Stocks Worth the Risk." Only a few of those passed muster, but they were goodies, let me tell you.

I also consulted a number of wise and knowledgeable people. Patrick McKeough sent me his top seven picks. Peter Winter, editor of *Canadian Biotech News*, was kind enough to send me his top 10 biotechnology picks. And I had the great pleasure of spending an hour and a half chatting with Brent Larsen and Ryan Irvine, the intrepid editors of *The FutureStock Review*. Some, but not all, of the stocks recommended by these gentlemen fit the criteria and are included in this collection.

After compiling an initial list of 88 possible companies, I checked out additional information on each stock through company websites and annual reports. Except for my chat with the fellows at *The FutureStock Review*, all of my research was done online. The Internet is an absolutely amazing resource for the investor. With stock lists, corporate websites, investing websites, and government databases, you can find out just about anything, as long as you stick to reputable sources.

It was not an easy project to select the 50 Best science and technology stocks. In fact, some allowances were made for ten stocks that did not meet all the requirements. The most common hurdle was the requirement for a stock to have only one year of negative return on invested capital. That's the same as only one year with reported losses. However, some companies had two or even three years of declining losses followed by two or more years of profits: Aastra Technologies, Arthrocare, and Magellan were included based on solid performance since entering the black. Internet Security Systems experienced two years of losses prior to going public as well as one afterwards. Zenon Technologies also failed on EPS growth, due to a loss in 2000 from increased capital spending, but I believe the company is poised to turn around in 2001. ATI Technologies also lost money in 2000 but met all the other growth standards. CAE Inc.'s revenues showed a marked drop in 1995 due to restructuring, but have grown steadily since. Wescam has steadily increased its earnings and revenues, but its share price has lagged considerably and came in below the 10 percent annual growth standard—in my opinion, this means the stock is undervalued. Video game company THQ Inc. underwent drastic restructuring in February 1995, consolidating shares on a one-for-15 basis. It had two years of losses before that and at one point was trading at a much higher share value and posting higher earnings per share. I based the star ratings and analysis for this company on its performance since 1995. Finally, BCE Inc. is a special case because it distributed its substantial interest in Nortel to shareholders in 2000, so the company's prior numbers are not comparable to its current financial performance.

Who Isn't Here

A quick note on stocks left out of this book: You'll note, for instance, that Canada's largest company, Nortel Networks, is not included.

Based on past history, it actually qualified, but you've read the news—
dramatic downturn in sales, massive layoffs, huge losses. It may be a
good candidate for next year's edition of the 50 Best, and a brave soul
might have included Nortel this year on the argument that the company is too big to fail. It is a market leader and should recover as the
economy recovers. And heck, you're never going to see Nortel this
cheap again. For me, prudence is the better part of valour.

I also left out a number of other well-known large technology companies—Cisco, Sun Microsystems, Oracle—preferring to focus on
younger upstarts such as Comverse and Mercury Interactive. The
older companies are not bad choices, but I feel that the younger companies can probably run a little faster in the short to medium haul.

Even though I made occasional allowances, many interesting companies still did not meet the selection criteria and couldn't be included.
Among them are the best of the networking companies, Juniper
Networks (JNPR-Q). It's taking market share in the core router business away from Cisco in a big way, but the company has been trading
publicly only since 1999, and doesn't have enough of a track record
to feature here. Similarly, nVidia (NVDA-Q) has been a huge success
in the video graphics chip market, steadily eroding ATI Technologies'
lead, but the company has also not been public for three years.

Other companies didn't make the cut due to poor past performance.
Genesis Microchip (GNSS-Q) shows real promise in the digital imaging field. Its chips go into most of the new flatbed monitors and should
do extremely well as the world goes digital. Cygnal Technologies
(CYN-T), the fastest-growing company in Canada in 2000, specializes in broadband networks, an increasingly important field, but it
only began turning a profit two years ago, and its share price growth
did not meet the series' standards. Sierra Wireless (SW-T) was the
fastest-growing company in 1999. Its wireless modems are increasingly popular and, as mobile computing becomes more established,
the company will prosper.

And finally, Ballard Power (BLD-T). The company has been losing money every year since its inception, but this concept stock could well be the next Intel, Cisco, or Microsoft in its growth potential. It's developed a clean alternative to the internal combustion engine, a potentially huge market. But it would be imprudent to include Ballard or the others noted above in a book that emphasizes a balanced and conservative approach. Maybe you will see some or all of these companies in future editions.

The 50 Best companies you will find in this book vary from large multinationals to little-known, smaller companies that have been quietly growing revenues and earnings without much fanfare. Many of the Canadian stocks are international in scope, with large markets outside of Canada. Some do 80 percent or more of their business outside of Canada. With the exceptions noted, all of the companies in this book show a strong track record of revenues, earnings, and share price growth.

Using the Book Effectively

As noted in the discussion of the Fast 50, science and technology stocks can be very volatile, with strong gains or sharp declines in a very short period of time. You already know the NASDAQ dropped 67.9 percent between March 30, 2000, and March 30, 2001, but let's take a look at Canada.

One hundred thirty-three securities on the TSE hit new lows for the week ending March 30, 2001. Of those, over 75 percent were science and technology driven. They included a who's who of the Canadian science and technology scene. Some were even on the Fast 50 list. Many of these are excellent companies and some are included as stocks for your consideration in this book—for example, Research in Motion went down 85 percent, Celestica 68 percent, and Cognos 66 percent. Their slide does not mean they're bad stocks, just that the market considered them overvalued and brought them back to a more reasonable level. I do want to emphasize how quickly and how severely a stock can drop, which brings me to suggestions on using the book effectively.

1. Diversify

The first thing to consider is your risk tolerance and how much of your portfolio you want to devote to potential high flyers. I believe all investment plans, within the context of a balanced portfolio, should include some science and technology stocks, particularly if you are younger and years away from retirement. These companies, after all, are the ones that will drive the economy in the future. The other books in this series, *The 50 Best Stocks for Canadians* and *The 50 Best Small Cap Stocks for Canadians*, will give you insights into some of Canada's stellar companies in consumer goods and services, manufacturing, finance, resources, and utilities. Diversification across all these sectors is recommended. Science and technology stocks can fall into nearly all of those categories, except finance and resources. As I've already mentioned, I have, in fact, divided up the 50 Best stocks into five categories to make diversification within this niche possible as well.

These sub-sectors are not always in sync; some may be advancing while others are retreating. Investors who were mostly into communications and Internet-related technology in the first quarter of 2000, and who did not have a selling discipline, would have suffered devastating losses in the following year. But those who diversified, particularly if they diversified into energy and industrial technologies, would have fared quite well.

On the contrarian side, there are some who believe the opposite strategy is preferable—rather than diversify, consolidate. In *The Gorilla Game: An Investor's Guide to Picking Winners in High Technology*, Geoffrey Moore and his co-authors recommend buying several stocks that have a chance of dominating a technology sector, and then as the market develops and one company looks to be emerging as the winner, selling the other stocks to put all your money behind the winner. This philosophy is echoed by Robert Kiyosaki in his *Rich Dad's Guide to Investing:* "Most investors say diversify. The rich investor focuses."

I see merits in both approaches, but it's like comparing apples and oranges in a way. Mr. Moore is talking about consolidating within a specific niche. Mr. Kiyosaki is talking about specialization. Neither recommends putting all of your investment eggs in one basket. Diversify your portfolio across the various economic sectors. And diversify your technology holdings across the various technology categories.

2. Buy Right

Once you've decided how much of your portfolio to allocate to science and technology stocks, you don't want to just go out and buy all the stocks in this book willy-nilly. For one thing, circumstances may have changed considerably since the book was written.

For another, each stock will appeal to different investors for different reasons. Although we have laid down fairly conservative criteria for inclusion in the 50 Best, some of the companies are decidedly more conservative than others. There's a big difference between BCE, for example, a large blue chip with a solid revenue base trying to become a force in the Internet economy, and Research in Motion, a promising but volatile stock. The one might exhibit slow, steady growth, while the other might have dramatic ups and downs. Both are excellent companies with excellent prospects, but an investor with a low tolerance for volatility would be better off with BCE.

You may want to buy the more conservative, large cap picks—BCE, Thomson, DuPont Canada, Intel, Microsoft, Pfizer, Merck, Magna International, or Bombardier—to lock into your portfolio with a long-term horizon (although not to completely forget about). One of the other books in this series, *The 50 Best Stocks for Canadians*, focuses on these stocks across a wider range of sectors. Other stocks you'll want to monitor and perhaps sell after a time. Still others among the 50 Best may no longer be attractive for various reasons: high prices, changing markets, and so on. The commentary on each stock should give you some thoughts on whether it is suitable for you.

An excellent general approach to selecting growth stocks is the CANSLIM approach developed by William O'Neil, founder of *Investors Business Daily*, in his best-selling book *How to Make Money in Stocks*. The appeal of this approach is that it is based, not on theory, but on empirical observation. He studied the top-performing 500 stocks between 1953 and 1993, looking for common threads that distinguished the really big winners from the herd. These common characteristics were CANSLIM, an acronym that stands for:

- **Current Quarterly Earnings Growth.** Mr. O'Neil discovered that three-quarters of the top-performing stocks had current quarterly EPS growth of 70 percent before they began their huge advance. At any one time, only about 2 percent of all stocks listed for trading will show such growth, he says, recommending 18 to 20 percent as a minimum standard of growth.
- **Annual Earnings Growth.** EPS for each of the last five years should show growth over the previous year. The annual compounded growth rate should be at least 25 percent, but the higher the better. The average of all firms Mr. O'Neil studied was 24 percent a year, but this included the one out of four stocks that were turnaround situations.
- **News.** New products, new management, new highs—a new discovery, invention, patent, product, or management often sparks a significant price move. Ninety-five percent of the successes Mr. O'Neil discovered had some significant change before their run-up. His most interesting discovery was that a stock making new highs tends to go higher, and a stock making new lows tends to

go lower. This goes completely contrary to the general wisdom of "buy low, sell high," and most people resist it. They prefer to look for stocks that have gone down in price and are, supposedly, a bargain. The contrarian (and profitable) position is "buy high, sell higher." In particular, look for stocks making 52-week highs for the first time. Note that many of the companies included in this book have suffered severe price declines in the wake of the technology crash. But many will be approaching the anniversary of their market bottoms from the fall of 2001 through the spring and summer of 2002, and may well be hitting 52-week highs again as you read this.

- **Supply and Demand.** Simply put, the smaller the number of shares outstanding, the lower the supply, and the more any demand for the stock will move the price upwards. It's not rocket science. Mr. O'Neil says, and I agree wholeheartedly, "The law of supply and demand is more important than all the analyst opinions on Wall Street." He also points out that excessive stock splits (which increase the supply on the market) are not good for a stock's price. Stocks sometimes peak just after a split. Similarly, a company buying back its own shares (and reducing the supply on the market) is a good thing.

- **Leadership.** In any industry group, some stocks are clearly the leaders, moving ahead by leaps and bounds. Others are clearly laggards—slow, pokey stocks that just can't keep up. Go for the leaders, not the followers. A strong indicator, in this respect, is a stock's relative price strength—how well the stock is doing against the rest of the market. The measure is a percentile score, like those on SAT tests: a relative strength of 90 indicates the stock is outperforming 90 percent of the other stocks in the market. Mr. O'Neil publishes relative strength numbers for all stocks on the major American markets every week in *Investors Business Daily*.

Such data for Canadian stocks, however, are hard to come by. I publish the relative strength numbers for the top 500 stocks on the TSE every month-end on my Investing: Canada website (http://investingcanada.about.com).

- **Institutional Sponsorship.** Mr. O'Neil argues that stocks tend to have some institutional sponsorship before they make really big moves. That is, mutual funds, pension funds, insurance companies, and the like should be buying. They provide "big demand." On the other hand, he cautions against excessive sponsorship. By the time every institution owns a stock, he says, it may already be too late to make big profits.

- **Market Direction.** Of course, market direction is an important factor. The NASDAQ plunge pulled down many good stocks as well as flighty, speculative issues. Don't swim against the tide. Don't spit into the wind. You get the picture.

To a certain extent, that is the approach I've taken in selecting the stocks in this book, focusing primarily on annual earnings growth and leadership. What the reader will want to consider is current quarterly earnings growth, any news concerning the company, and perhaps market direction. It was pretty obvious what direction parts of the technology market were taking in 2000 and 2001, and people bucked the market at their peril. Like the old Bobby Fuller Four song says, "I Fought the Law and the Law Won." If you fight the market, the market will win.

3. Sell Right

Science and technology stocks can be among the fastest growing and also the most volatile stocks on the market. Consequently, it is worth having a selling plan in place to forestall severe losses (or the vaporization of your paper profits).

An excellent book on the subject is Donald Cassidy's *It's When You Sell That Counts*. A senior analyst with Lipper Analytical Services, he has years of experience observing and working in the markets. His most intriguing argument for having a selling plan is that holding a stock should be an active and not a passive decision. The buy-and-hold philosophy says pick a good stock, buy it, and forget about it. But, as Mr. Cassidy points out, even the most stalwart stock may falter at some point. Fundamentals change. Sometimes these are broad fundamentals, such as the changing nature of the economy. Sometimes these are fundamentals within an industry or even a specific company.

Consider the Dow Jones Industrial Average, the venerable measure of stock market performance launched by Charles Dow on May 26, 1896. It started with 12 stocks considered to be solid and representative of the broad market at the time. The Dow Jones Company says that in selecting stocks for the average, it looks "among substantial industrial companies with a history of successful growth and wide interest among investors." It is not a current hot stock list, as the listings are changed infrequently; the aim is "stability of composition."

The Dow was increased to 20 stocks in 1916 and to 30 stocks in 1928, the number it has stayed at ever since. But the same 30? No. In fact, only one stock in the current Dow has been around since 1896—General Electric. Several companies have been removed at some point and later reinstated. GE was removed and reinstated twice before 1928. U.S. Rubber, DuPont, and IBM are others that have been on the list more than once, with IBM removed in 1939 and not rejoining the index until 40 years later. Mr. Cassidy reports that half of the components of the Dow have changed since 1961. The most recent changes were in 1999 when Union Carbide, Sears Roebuck, Goodyear, and Chevron were removed in favour of Home Depot, Intel, Microsoft, and SBC Communications. The point is that these companies, supposedly the most stable and successful in the U.S., are constantly changing. In other words, even the Dow doesn't hold its stocks forever.

A buy-and-hold strategy is particularly problematic in the constantly changing world of technology. Consider the seven largest computer companies in 1984, when the industry was in its youth. Only IBM remains intact, though it underwent some painful problems, including a long-running antitrust battle and the transition from large mainframes to PCs. This supposedly unstoppable dynamo of a stock at one point took a 75 percent hit on its share price, though it is now doing very well again. The other six—Burroughs, Sperry, NCR, Digital Equipment, Honeywell, and Control Data—either merged, were taken over by other companies, or changed the nature of their business. All are considered minor players today.

So what selling strategies should the science and technology investor have in place? That depends on the nature of the company and current market conditions, but here are a few suggestions:

- If the stock doubles, consider selling half, particularly if the stock is more speculative. At the same time, you don't want to lose out on potential future gains. So consider this option in conjunction with other factors.
- Sell when fundamentals falter. If a previously profitable company comes in with a bad earnings report or sales are dropping off, put yourself on alert. If it comes in with a second, sell if you haven't already done so.
- Sell when trends shift. This was a good tip when the NASDAQ started faltering. Market indices are trend indicators. Some stocks can buck a trend, but beware and be prepared.
- Watch for a blow-off top. Sometimes stocks will experience a sudden and dramatic upswing in price. This is often unsustainable, and you may want to be nimble and take quick profits. Then, if the stock still exhibits the fundamentals that made you buy it in the first place, buy back after it drops down in price again.
- Cut your losses short. The full saying is "Cut your losses short and let your winners run," or in other words, set a point below which you will not tolerate further losses. The editors of the *Cabot Market Letter*, who specialize in growth stocks and use

a combination of momentum and fundamentals to select their stocks, recommend selling if any stock gives you a 15 to 20 percent loss. Others recommend a 10 percent limit. But another excellent suggestion is discussed below.

Channel Surfing for Fun and Profit

We're not talking about sitting in front of the tube like a couch potato here. We're talking about stock chart channels. In *It's When You Sell That Counts*, Mr. Cassidy notes that stock prices don't move in a straight line. They go up. They go down. They go up again. On a graph, a stock price makes a zigzag pattern, which can trend upwards, downwards, or sideways.

Mr. Cassidy does not like the idea of setting some arbitrary point at which to cut your losses based on your purchase price. Rather, he says you should note the stock's recent history. Suppose you buy a stock that is in a general upwards trend. Drawing roughly parallel lines connecting the outer edges of the stock's fluctuations gives us a price channel. As long as its zigzagging prices stay roughly within the parameters of its channel—its general trend—you should hold on to it. When it clearly breaches the channel, in either direction, you should be prepared for the possibility of selling. If the channel is breached on the upside by a sharp spike accompanied by heavy volume, you are witnessing a possible blow-off top and should consider selling. If the channel is breached on the downside, note any previous resistance points and watch to see if they are breached as well. If so, sell.

For example, Calpine is one of the stocks recommended in this book. I became so enamoured of the stock when writing about it that I bought some, just as it neared the top of an up-channel. When the stock fell, I didn't heed my own advice because I got trapped in a common error investors make—don't fall in love with your stock! Calpine is growing at a tremendous rate. There's a huge energy crisis in California. How can it lose? Or so I reasoned. So I bought some more after it had fallen well below the sell point. And it fell further!

If I had followed my own advice here, I would have sold the stock when it broke below its trend lines and kept the money on the sidelines waiting for a good buying opportunity (since I still liked the company's story and its fundamentals). I would then have had more stock to profit from when the stock price recovered. The cause of the stock's fall, by the way, was concern that Calpine might not be able to secure payment from its virtually bankrupt California customers—big utilities such as Pacific Gas and Electric, which bought power from Calpine to resell to consumers at a loss under California's bungled deregulation scheme.

How Important Is the Price/Earnings Ratio?

Value investors are wont to disparage science and technology stocks because they often sport high price/earnings ratios. That is a mistake. P/E ratios vary from industry to industry and sector to sector. Industries that are growing quickly will have higher P/E ratios because expectations of future gain are built into today's stock price.

The same is true of rapidly growing companies. Consider a company that is growing earnings at 100 percent a year. The average P/E ratio for the industry is, say, 18. But company X has a P/E of 72, because of the expectation of continued profit growth. If the company keeps growing at the same rate and the stock price stays the same, the P/E will be down to 18 in two years. As long as the expectation of continued growth is not dampened, the stock price will continue to grow and the P/E will stay high. Microsoft sported a high P/E of 61.0, 69.3, and 71.0 in 1998, 1999, and 2000. Its low P/E in the latter two years never dropped below 31. But Microsoft was growing earnings at 34.8 percent, 55.1 percent, and 22.5 percent for those years. The stock price appreciated from US$31.59 at its fiscal year-end in 1997 to US$80.00 at the close of fiscal 2000, a gain of 153.2 percent.

True, some of the valuations during the technology mania of 1999–2000 saw stocks with no profits at all going through the roof.

P/Es in the hundreds were not uncommon (and still aren't). So how can you tell if a P/E ratio is too high? Consider a company with a P/E of 500, in an industry where the norm is, say, 25. The company is growing earnings at 50 percent a year. For the company to reach the industry average P/E, with a constant stock price, it would have to continue growing at that pace for eight and a half years. Extrapolate the current EPS to see if that is realistic. If the company is earning a dollar a share this year, is it reasonable to expect it to earn over $20 a share in eight and a half years?

Moreover, we're talking about the stock treading water for eight and half years to let its EPS catch up. Who wants to hold a stock that stays flat for so long? In order for a stock to appreciate while its P/E goes down, earnings have to be growing faster than the share price is growing, or else you'll have a bubble, and ultimately, bubbles burst.

There is a natural limit to growth, but such high P/E ratios might be justified when the company is earning just pennies a share. An example is Ebay, one of the few Internet companies that actually turned a profit in 1998. In November of that year, the stock was trading around US$125, with earnings of just four and a half cents a share. Its P/E ratio was an astounding 2800. Ebay has split six-for-one since. Split-adjusted, the stock then was only US$21 with earnings of three-quarters of a cent. In mid-2001, Ebay was trading at US$60. Its earnings had mushroomed to 30 cents a share, and its P/E ratio had dropped to 205. Was Ebay too expensive with a P/E ratio of 2800? Investors who bought then have tripled their money, even though Ebay is off 50 percent from its all-time high. Is it too high now with a P/E of 205? (Ebay, by the way, is not included in this book since it is an auction house and not a technology company. But it would certainly qualify on performance criteria.)

Below is a table of a $5.00 stock earning just $0.01 a share with a projected earnings growth rate of 50 percent a year.

Year	Price	EPS	P/E
0	$ 5.00	$ 0.01	500
1	$ 5.00	$ 0.015	333.3
2	$ 5.00	$ 0.02	222.2
3	$ 5.00	$ 0.03	148.2
4	$ 5.00	$ 0.05	98.8
5	$ 5.00	$ 0.08	65.8
6	$ 5.00	$ 0.11	43.9
7	$ 5.00	$ 0.17	29.3
8	$ 5.00	$ 0.26	19.5
9	$ 5.00	$ 0.38	13.0
10	$ 5.00	$ 0.58	8.7
11	$ 5.00	$ 0.86	5.8
12	$ 5.00	$ 1.30	3.9

As you can see, the P/E ratio drops quickly as earnings mount. You, as an investor, have to decide whether the projected growth and earnings expectations are realistic—what are the EPS of comparable companies? We're starting with an EPS of just a penny in the table. But if a company is already earning a dime a share and has a P/E of 500, that means it is expected to earn $2.80 a share in eight years if it stands still in price. Is that a reasonable expectation?

On the other hand, if a company's earnings start falling faster than its stock price, a situation many companies were facing in the first half of 2001, failure to recover could mean the stock will plunge even further. Just as fast-growing earnings are the salvation and justification of a stock with a high P/E ratio, quickly sliding earnings can be the kiss of death. An accurate assessment of a company's earnings growth prospects can be crucial.

There are just over 15,000 stocks in North America, and just over 200 stocks with P/E ratios of 100 or more. They include some of the fastest-growing companies on the continent. So the importance you put on P/E depends on the context. How high is the P/E? What are the company's current earnings per share? What is its growth rate?

Through a Glass, Brightly

Science and technology is a fascinating subject. The world is changing faster now than ever before. Who would have thought 35 years ago that in 15 years you would be able to telephone your spouse from your car? Who would have thought 15 years ago that in five years you'd be able to transmit written messages live over a new invention called the Internet? Who would have thought five years ago that in two years you'd be able to download all your favourite music from when you were a kid? Who would have thought two years ago that...? Your guess is as good as mine.

Richard McGinn, former CEO of Lucent Technologies said, "You either move with speed or die. It's the converse of 'speed kills.'" Lucent didn't move fast enough to keep pace with Nortel, and it's dying. McGinn no longer works there. And we're not 100 percent sure about Nortel. How can you, a regular investor, keep up with it all? The answer is, you can't. That said, there are some broad trends that investors can consider in making investment decisions:

- **Convergence.** This theme of technology guru Nicholas Negroponte is fast becoming reality. Examples related to the stocks in this book are the acquisition of the CTV television network by BCE and the merger of America Online with Time Warner. In the near future, television, radio, newspapers, magazines, and the Internet will be one merged entity—the media. As an investor, look for companies that are capitalizing on this trend.
- **Outsourcing.** In an increasingly competitive world, companies are trying to cut costs while maintaining quality in production. The result is that they are focusing on their core competencies and outsourcing the rest. For example, in June 2001, Laurentian Bank

decided to outsource its IT functions to CGI Group. Laurentian's core competency is banking. Why maintain an extensive IT department when CGI can do it better and more cheaply? So, look for companies that provide services to companies that are outsourcing. Others included among the 50 Best are Patheon, Trican Well Services, Magna, Tesma, Solectron, Celestica, and C-MAC Industries.

- **Wireless.** The wired world will remain an important part of the telecommunications infrastructure, but wireless will gain increasing importance over the years ahead. Cellular phones are already tremendously popular, but they are nowhere near saturation level. Look for companies that can tap into this market, such as Research in Motion.

- **The Internet.** Despite the demise of many dot-coms, the Internet will become increasingly important in the years ahead, particularly in business. Look for companies that are facilitating e-commerce in particular, such as Siebel, Cognos, or Mercury Interactive, all included in this book.

- **Nanotechnology.** Things will get smaller and smaller. Flatbed computer screens and television screens will become common. Companies involved in video technology that are featured in this book include Wescam and Silent Witness.

- **Energy.** U.S. consumption of electricity is growing by 3 percent a year, and energy will be a growth industry in all its facets in the years to come. Power companies and technical support services for resource companies will continue to be in high demand. And environmental concerns will continue to fuel demand for alternative energy technology. You will find four great companies in the Energy section.

- **Medical breakthroughs.** An aging population will place even more demands on our health care system. There will be increasing urgency to develop cures for diseases associated with aging.

Seek out pharmaceutical companies with established products and large research and development budgets, as well as medical outsourcing companies, all of which you will find in the Biology, Medicine, and Environment section.

To keep up with future trends and ideas, here are a few handy online resources:

- The Future File (www.futurefile.com): Canadian broadcaster and futurist Tod Maffin's website
- Dr. Tomorrow (www.drtomorrow.com): Another Canadian futurist, Frank Ogden
- Canadian Biotech News (www.canadianbiotechnews.com)
- MIT Technology Review (www.technologyreview.com)
- Red Herring (www.redherring.com)
- Wired (www.wired.com)

Using the Internet To Research a Stock

The overviews in this book are short—500 to 625 words each. I've tried to make them interesting and informative, but it is difficult to do a company justice in such a short space. The historical financial data in each profile will be difficult to find anywhere else, but before you invest, you will also want a sense of the current state of the company. If my discussion gives you an interest in a particular stock, check it out further.

Nearly all the research for this book was done online using the Internet. It is an impressive resource, but using it effectively can be a challenge. Company websites are listed in each 50 Best profile so that you can read further about the company's business and management. Many corporate websites have two-page fact sheets that offer a quick overview. Then go to the Investors or Financials section and download the most recent annual report. Nearly every company now has its annual report available online in PDF format, often several years' worth. Some corporate sites also include analyst reports. If so, check them out. Corporate websites are usually the best sources for in-depth studies, but their quality does vary.

General investing websites such as Globeinvestor.com and Advice for Investors are excellent for quick and easy access to key information. Let me conclude with a list of handy websites you can use to do your own research. Go to town. Have fun.

General Resources
* Investing: Canada at About.com (http://investingcanada. about.com): My own website, which links to all the resources below.
* Globeinvestor.com (www.globeinvestor.com): The best all-around investing website. You can check out company profiles, three-year performance statistics, and stock charts. The News section for each stock features headlines, including recent quarterly reports where you can check how a company is doing in the short term.
* Advice for Investors (www.adviceforinvestors.com): Formerly called Carlson Online, this site includes links to news from the major wire services, to Sedar profiles and documents, and to company websites. Go for the free service.
* Equity Research Center (www.equityresearchcenter.com)
* Sedar (www.sedar.com): The government's corporate document database, Sedar is the repository for all mandatory company filings, including annual reports.
* Toronto Stock Exchange (www.tse.com)
* Big Charts (www.bigcharts.com): The best site for historical pricing information—use the prefix CA: for Canadian stocks.
* Canadian Shareowner (www.shareowner.com): Home of the Stock Study Guide, a subscription service.

Stock Lists

- Re$earch Infosource (www.researchinfosource.com/new/top100.html): Lists the top 100 companies for R&D spending in Canada.
- Fast 50 (www.deloitte.ca/en/Industries/TechComm/Fast50/default.asp)
- Fast 500 (www.us.deloitte.com/fast500/index.shtm)
- Branham 300 (www.branham.ca/branham300/index.php)
- Profit 100 (www.profitguide.com/profit100)
- Fortune 100 (www.fortune.com): Select Fastest-Growing 100 from the drop-down menu.
- T-Net 100 (www.bctechnology.com/frameset_tnet100.html)
- Alberta's Fastest Growing Companies (www.albertaventure.com/best)

Newsletters

- The Successful Investor (www.thesuccessfulinvestor.com)
- The FutureStock Review (www.keystocks.com)
- The Cabot Market Letter (www.cabot.net)
- Addicted to Profits (www.addictedtoprofits.com): This newsletter is not science or technology oriented but offers interesting observations on the economy and stock markets.

How the Book Is Arranged

You'll find the stocks in this book arranged by broad market sector: Biology, Medicine, and Environment; Energy; Industry; Information Technology; and Telecommunications. The number of stocks in each varies from a low of four in the Energy category to a high of 18 in the IT section.

Each profile begins with the basic facts about the company and its management. A short table gives the stock a rating of up to five stars on each of three measurable growth criteria: revenue, EPS, and share price. Here's how the star ratings were assigned: The minimum average growth rates for inclusion in the book were 5 percent annual revenue growth, 5 percent annual EPS growth, and 10 percent annual share price growth over the last 10 years. Using my trusty spreadsheet program, I calculated that 5 percent annual growth for 10 years was equivalent to a total 62.89 percent increase. Ten percent meant 159.4 percent cumulative change. Fifteen percent annually translated to 304.6 percent, 20 percent to 519.2 percent, and 25 percent to 831.3 percent.

Since we're looking for big growth with science and technology, I decided that achieving 5 percent growth in any category warranted one star; 10 percent, two stars; 15 percent, three stars; 20 percent, four stars; and 25 percent, five stars. Then I calculated the percentage increases from 10 years ago to the most recent complete fiscal year and awarded stars accordingly. For younger companies with less than 10 years' history, I used the data from the first available year as the starting point. So a six-year-old company with three stars in, say, revenue growth, actually grew at significantly greater than 15 percent annual growth to achieve an increase of 304.6 percent in its sales. This balanced out the fact that companies often grow much faster in their early years with the lack of a longer track record. The number of stars for revenue, EPS, and share price growth were then added to get an overall star rating.

Following the ratings table is general company background, followed by two sections. "Opportunities and Challenges" looks at the reasons I expect the stock to grow and discusses any negatives facing the company that may add risk to the investment. "Financial Highlights" identifies the more important developments reflected in the financial table that closes the profile and shows a company's results over the past 10 years.

About Me

Since 1997, I have been the guide for Investing: Canada at About.com, the sixth most popular web portal in North America, according to Media Metrix. During the Internet boom, I created a Canadian Internet Index and profiled many Canadian Internet stocks. Now I'm profiling stocks that have hit new highs and are generating solid earnings growth.

I have no professional connection with any brokerage house or vested interest relating to the stocks reviewed in this book. However, I may own, may have owned, or may own any of them in the future. Specifically, at the time of writing I have owned or own the following stocks: ATI, BCE, CAE, EMC, THQ (okay, I like alphabet soup!), Biovail, Canadian Medical Laboratories, Calpine, Cree, Gennum, Microsoft, Siebel, Thomson Corporation, and Wescam. If I could afford to and it didn't spread me too thin, I'd own a piece of all 50 of these fine companies.

Philosophically, I am a hardcore fan of capitalism and its blessings. Preparing this book, I was filled with awe and admiration for the achievements of the people behind these companies—people such as J. Armande Bombardier, who loved machines and tinkered in his shop to invent the snowmobile; Robert Noyce and Gordon Moore, who followed their vision and made the modern world of computers possible; Serge Godin and André Imbeau, who turned a small Quebec City business consultancy into a billion-dollar powerhouse; Bill Gates, who dropped out of university to develop Microsoft; K. Y. Ho, who peddled vegetables as a child in Communist China, but founded the world's leading graphics card company after immigrating to Canada; Christopher Klaus, who at 18 invented the security program that became the basis for Internet Security Systems; Klaus Woerner, who immigrated to Canada and started ATS Automation Tooling Systems; and Frank Stronach, who turned a small machine shop into a multi-billion-dollar automotive empire. There are many, many more.

I was a university student in the late 1960s, when self-styled revolutionaries were setting fires on campuses, rioting, and hoping to change the world. But the world has been changed as much if not more by technology and the products and services it enables. In 1974, when the microprocessor was just beginning to have an impact, Intel founder Gordon Moore said, "I'd like to think that we're the real revolutionaries in the world. Things are being revolutionized a lot more by electronics technology than by some political things going on."

So read on about the true revolutionaries. Enjoy.

BIOLOGY, MEDICINE, AND ENVIRONMENT

Biovail Corporation
Patheon Inc.
Axcan Pharma Inc.
Forest Laboratories, Inc.
Pfizer Inc.
ArthroCare Corporation
MDS Inc.
Merck & Company, Inc.
Canadian Medical Laboratories Ltd.
Zenon Environmental Inc.

BIOVAIL CORPORATION

2488 Dunwin Drive
Mississauga, ON L5L 1J9

Tel: (416) 285-6000   Employees: 1,200
Fax: (416) 285-6499   Listed: 1987
www.biovail.com
Symbol: BVF (TSE) (Also NYSE)

Chairperson: Eugene N. Melnyk
CEO: Bruce D. Brydon

Share Price Growth	★ ★ ★ ★ ★
Revenue Growth	★ ★ ★ ★ ★
EPS Growth	★ ★ ★ ★
BVF	**14**

About the Company

Unlike drug companies that focus on developing new proprietary
drugs, Biovail has focused on drug delivery systems, specifically, oral
controlled-release technologies. The company applies these patented
technologies to existing medications to develop new branded and
generic products.

Controlled-release products are a significant improvement over
the same medicine taken say, three times a day. They offer more pre-
dictable drug delivery throughout the day, as well as obviating the
problem of patients forgetting to take their medicine. Biovail targets

successful multiple dosage drugs to create improved once-a-day versions, and it also creates generic versions of drugs whose patents have expired.

The company has commercialized more than 20 different products in Canada, the U.S., and over 55 other countries. American sales are handled through strategic partners, Forest Laboratories and Teva Pharmaceuticals. Sixteen further products are in the research and development stage.

An important part of Biovail is its contract research organization. Its five departments design pharmaceutical studies for clients and carry them through to clinical trials. The company's two clinics in downtown Toronto house 230 beds to accommodate a great variety of studies. Equipped with state-of-the-art analytical tools, Biovail Contract Research has been involved in research on dozens of drugs, including the AIDS drug, acyclovir.

Biovail was the 20th-largest spender on R&D in Canada in 2000 according to Re$earch Infosource.

Opportunities and Challenges

The oral controlled-release pharmaceutical market offers some unique growth opportunities. Biovail has six different controlled-release technology platforms, which give it the flexibility to customize a wide variety of drugs regardless of their physical, chemical, or clinical properties.

The company has been successful in buying expiring patents from their current owners, then developing a new oral, controlled-release form of the patented drug. New patents can then be applied for. This process has served to extend the life of a number of patents and forestalled generic competition on these drugs.

Two significant acquisitions in 2000 will add to Biovail's strength and market presence. The acquisition of DJ Pharma in October gives it a sales force of 300 south of the border, enabling the company to sell directly into the U.S. market, rather than just through licensing agreements. The acquisition of the rights to Cardizem from Aventis Pharmaceuticals gives it the world's best-selling diltiazem product for hypertension and angina. Combined with its existing Tiazac line, Biovail should dominate the market for this medication.

Biovail has been successful in extending the patent lifespan of existing drugs through modification, but a possible reversal on the status of its number-one product, Tiazac, could open the way for generic competition from competitor, Andrx Corporation. Tiazac contributed 30 percent of sales in 2000. Biovail has its own generic version of the drug in the pipeline, however, and this should mitigate any loss of market share.

The company has been involved in a number of lawsuits, as both plaintiff and defendant, over patent infringement. Although Biovail has prevailed in litigation so far, adverse court decisions could impact the company.

The quarter to March 31, 2001 showed a 135 percent increase in revenues and an 82 percent increase in earnings year-over-year.

Financial Highlights

The company has shown consistent, strong revenue growth, with exceptional growth in 2000. This was driven by soaring sales of Tiazac and the launch of four new generic products which generated strong sales in the U.S. and Canada. The decline in earnings for 2000 was due to a one-time charge related to a change in accounting principles, as well as a 50 percent increase in R&D spending. The share price has fluctuated in 2000 and 2001 depending on the status of patent litigation. The overall long-term trend, however, is upwards.

Biovail Corporation at a Glance

Fiscal Year-end: December

7-Year Return: 89.5%

	1996	1997	1998	1999	2000	8-Year Growth Average (%)	Total (%)
Revenue ($ mlns.)	80.4	99.8	155.6	219.2	437.6	69.6	2,876.9
Net Income ($ mlns.)	31.9	50.3	69.8	77.8	53.1	–	–
Earnings/ Share ($)	0.29	0.47	0.63	0.76	0.37	–	–
Dividend/ Share ($)	–	–	–	–	–	–	–
Price/ Earnings	24.1 - 47	15.1 - 30	12.7 - 27.9	15.6 - 45	74.3 - 187.8	–	–

Table data courtesy of *Canadian Shareowner* **www.shareowner.com**

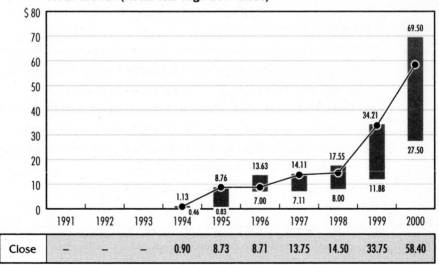

Stock Growth (Fiscal Year High-Low-Close)

| Close | – | – | – | 0.90 | 8.73 | 8.71 | 13.75 | 14.50 | 33.75 | 58.40 |

PATHEON INC.

2100 Syntex Court
Mississauga, ON L5N 7K9

Tel: (905) 821-4001   Employees: 1,935
Fax: (905) 812-6705   Founded: 1974
www.patheon.com   Listed: 1981
Symbol: PTI (TSE)

CEO and CFO: Robert C. Tedford

Share Price Growth	★ ★ ★ ★ ★
Revenue Growth	★ ★ ★ ★
EPS Growth	★ ★ ★
PTI	**12**

About the Company

Patheon provides manufacturing and contract research facilities for the pharmaceutical and biotechnology industries. With five plants in the Toronto area as well as three in Europe, the company serves over 100 clients, including 13 of the 20 largest pharmaceutical companies in the world. This impressive client list includes such giants as Hoffman-La Roche, SmithKline Beecham, Bristol-Myers Squibb, Johnson & Johnson, Bayer, and Pfizer.

The company has a long history, founded in 1974 in Fort Erie, Ontario. It moved to Burlington in 1981 and started serving the U.S. market in 1990. Since then, the company has grown internally and through acquisition. The company's goal is to become the dominant player in pharmaceutical outsourcing.

In 2000, 68 percent of the company's revenues came from pre-scription drug manufacturing, 24 percent from over-the-counter medications, and the balance from contract research. Products made by Patheon are sold in over 100 countries.

Opportunities and Challenges

As patents expire and demand for new drugs increases, many pharma-ceutical companies are focusing their efforts on R&D and marketing. They are increasingly outsourcing manufacturing to third parties such as Patheon. The American market for outsourced drug manufactur-ing, in fact, is growing at 10 to 12 percent a year.

On top of that, the number of biotechnology companies has doubled in the last five years. These companies are research-focused and look-ing for ways to bring their products to market without expensive out-lays for manufacturing facilities. The solution? Again, it is outsourcing.

These trends have created tremendous growth opportunities for Patheon. Revenues have skyrocketed 683.7 percent in the last five years, doubling between 1999 and 2000 alone. And earnings per share have grown fivefold in the last six years, almost doubling in 2000.

The company has taken advantage of opportunities to grow by ac-quisition as well, buying manufacturing facilities from Upjohn Canada, Hoffman-La Roche in both Canada and Italy, Hoechst Marion Roussel in Britain, and Bourguin-Jallieu in France. These takeovers invariably included long-term contracts to continue manufacturing products for the companies selling their plants.

As with outsourcing companies in the electronics arena (such as Celestica and C-MAC), Patheon's success depends on the health and success of its clients. Much of Patheon's growth was fuelled by the ac-quisition of plants from companies that are now its customers. With such growth comes the risk that contracts won't be renewed at the ex-piration of current contracts.

But that raises the question: Why did the client companies sell their plants in the first place? There is economic advantage to outsourcing, including minimizing investment in costly facilities and focusing on core competencies of R&D and marketing. These advantages are not likely to disappear when current contracts end, and Patheon has a broad and diversified clientele.

The first half of fiscal 2001 showed continued growth for Patheon, with a 14 percent increase in revenues and a 26.7 percent increase in earnings per share over the same period the year before. Operating margins also increased, reflecting increased volume of business spread over the same fixed costs. However, the pace of growth slowed on a quarterly basis.

Financial Highlights

The company's stock price suffered a bit during the technology downturn, but for the most part held its value. The stock traded in a broad range from $12.00 to $16.50 from September 2000 through July 2001. Continued growth in revenues and earnings should propel it to new highs in 2002. Value investor Jonathan Wellum of AIC Diversified Canada Fund reported in June 2001 that he had added Patheon as a solid pick in a weak economy, with potential for growth on economic recovery. He also sees it as a potential takeover candidate.

Patheon Inc. at a Glance

Fiscal Year-end: October

6-Year Return: 65.5%

	1996	1997	1998	1999	2000	6-Year Growth Average (%)	Total (%)
Revenue ($ mlns.)	38.5	50.7	70.5	127.4	256.3	54.1	683.8
Net Income ($ mlns.)	2.2	2.4	4.0	7.3	13.6	60.7	871.4
Earnings/ Share ($)	0.10	0.07	0.12	0.18	0.31	46.1	416.7
Dividend/ Share ($)	–	–	–	–	–	–	–
Price/ Earnings	8.3 - 18	18.6 - 40	16.3 - 28.2	15.6 - 66.4	20.5 - 54.4	–	–

Table data courtesy of **Canadian Shareowner** **www.shareowner.com**

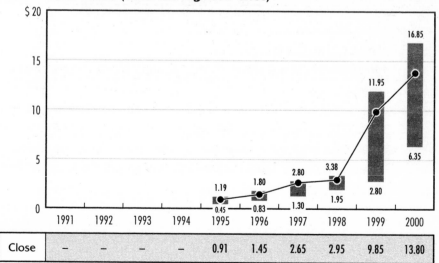

Stock Growth (Fiscal Year High-Low-Close)

	1991	1992	1993	1994	1995	1996	1997	1998	1999	2000
Close	–	–	–	–	0.91	1.45	2.65	2.95	9.85	13.80

AXCAN PHARMA INC.

597 Laurier Blvd.
Mont St. Hilaire, QC J3H 6C4

Tel: (450) 467-5138   Employees: 1,500
Fax: (450) 464-9979   Founded: 1982
www.axcan.com   Listed: 1995
Symbol: AXP (TSE) (Also AXCA-NASDAQ)

President and CEO: Leon Gosselin
Executive VP and COO: David W. Mims

Share Price Growth	★
Revenue Growth	★ ★ ★ ★ ★
EPS Growth	★ ★ ★ ★ ★
AXP	**11**

About the Company

Quebec-based Axcan Pharma is the leading North American pharmaceutical company in the field of gastroenterology. Founded in 1982 as Interfalk by Leon Gosselin and Dr. Herbert Falk, the company launched its first product, Salofalk, a treatment for ulcerative colitis, in 1986.

A year later, the company began a research collaboration with the Mayo Clinic on the treatment of primary biliary cirrhosis with ursodiol. Axcan's drug Urso was approved by the FDA in December 1997, giving Axcan the distinction of being one of only four Canadian companies ever to have received approval for an innovative drug from the FDA.

Over the years, Axcan acquired a number of non-prescription gastrointestinal medications to complement the company's lines. These include several drugs from Wyeth-Ayerst and Jouveinal Inc.

Axcan has also adopted a strategy of acquiring gastrointestinal-related products in the late stages of development from other companies. It then completes the clinical trials and brings them to market. One product so acquired is Photofrin, a light-activated treatment for esophageal cancers and Barrett's esophagus purchased from QLT Phototherapeutics. Photofrin is already approved for use in 11 European countries and is awaiting approval for the U.S. market.

Axcan acquired American company Scandipharm in 1999, becoming the first Canadian drug company with its own U.S. national sales force. The company is now poised for its next stage of significant growth.

Leon Gosselin was honoured as Quebec's Entrepreneur of the Year in September 2000 for his outstanding leadership in the health sciences field. Axcan was added to the TSE 300 in 2000, and is dual traded in U.S. dollars on the NASDAQ exchange.

Opportunities and Challenges

The company now has two prescription drugs onstream, with Photofrin in the registration phase in the U.S. Five more drugs are in phase three of clinical trials for treatment of nine disorders, and Axcan's portfolio of related drugs acquired from other companies includes treatments for cystic fibrosis.

To foster the company's growth, it brought in David Mims in March 2000 as executive vice-president and chief operating officer. Mr. Mims has years of experience with drug companies in the United States, including seven years with Scandipharm. Axcan Pharma's revenues more than doubled in 2000, and there is every indication similar growth lies ahead. Axcan is a small company compared to some of the pharmaceutical giants of the U.S. and Europe. Its challenge will be to keep growing and keep focused on its niche market, where it is a recognized leader.

Eighty percent of Axcan's revenues are generated in the U.S., which helps insulate the company from declines in the Canadian dollar, and also gives the stock upside potential from a deteriorating exchange rate.

Axcan Pharma had a superb quarterly report to March 31, 2001, with revenues up 58 percent and earnings per share moving to a 7-cent profit from a 3-cent loss the year before.

Financial Highlights

Axcan Pharma was thinly traded prior to January 2000, and its share price fluctuated widely. But since then it has had strong volume and moved up steadily from $6.00 to a peak of $18.50, before settling into a broad range from $13.50 to $18.00. That narrowed to a range from $16.50 to $18.00 after May 2001. The stock was basing in mid-2001 and should be ready to break out if revenues and earnings continue to show strength.

Axcan Pharma Inc. at a Glance

Fiscal Year-end: September

5-Year Return: 11.9%

	1996	1997	1998	1999	2000	6-Year Growth Average (%)	6-Year Growth Total (%)
Revenue ($ mlns.)	16.1	18.8	42.6	63.3	131.8	61.8	790.5
Net Income ($ mlns.)	0.1	-1.3	0.6	2.2	7.4	–	–
Earnings/ Share ($)	0.01	-0.09	0.04	0.14	0.27	–	–
Dividend/ Share ($)	–	–	–	–	–	–	–
Price/ Earnings	500 - 1080	-108.3 - -167.8	250 - 362.5	47.1 - 76.4	21.3 - 68.5	–	–

Table data courtesy of **Canadian Shareowner   www.shareowner.com**

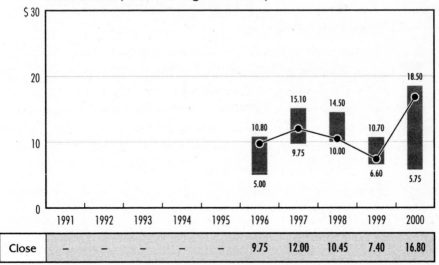

Stock Growth (Fiscal Year High-Low-Close)

	1991	1992	1993	1994	1995	1996	1997	1998	1999	2000
Close	–	–	–	–	–	9.75	12.00	10.45	7.40	16.80

FOREST LABORATORIES, INC.

909 Third Avenue
New York, NY 10022

Tel: (212) 421-7850   Employees: 2,500
www.frx.com   Founded: 1956
Symbol: FRX (NYSE)   Listed: 1967

Chairperson and CEO: Howard Solomon
President and COO: Kenneth E. Goodman

Share Price Growth	★ ★ ★ ★
Revenue Growth	★ ★ ★ ★
EPS Growth	★ ★ ★
FRX	**11**

About the Company

You snooze, you lose! That old saying applies to many of the large, established drug companies in America. They snoozed, and Forest Labs won in a big way. What did it gain? Celexa, a selective serotonin reuptake inhibitor (SSRI) developed by the Danish pharmaceutical firm H. Lundbeck, that competes effectively with such antidepressants as Prozac, Zoloft, and Paxil.

None of the companies with the resources to outbid Forest Labs for the U.S. rights to Celexa nibbled, fearing the market was overcrowded. But Forest CEO Howard Solomon acquired Celexa in 1998. Through an aggressive and focused sales force, Forest turned it into one of the fastest-growing drugs in America. It now commands 12 percent of the SSRI market.

The drug is differentiated by faster action, less conflict with other drugs, higher response rate, and fewer side effects. In fact, many think it is the best of the antidepressants, and its market share could grow significantly larger.

Forest Laboratories is an old, well-established drug company with a different approach to R&D. As one analyst put it, its strategy is "minimal R and lots of D." What Forest does (and does extremely well) is negotiate licensing deals for drugs developed by other, often smaller, companies that lack the resources to finish research and bring their products to market.

A good part of its business comes from introducing successful foreign drugs to the American market by shepherding them through the FDA approval process, or serving as the U.S. marketing arm for these products. Celexa is a prime example. Another is the hypertension and angina medication Tiazac, manufactured by Canada's Biovail and marketed in the U.S. by Forest.

Forest Labs is growing profits at 35 percent a year, far higher than the industry average of 15 percent, and commands a correspondingly high valuation. It was 23rd on *Fortune's* 2000 list of the fastest growing companies in America and topped a billion dollars U.S. in sales in fiscal 2001.

Opportunities and Challenges

Forest Labs has a number of products in its production pipeline, including Escitalopram, an improved version of Celexa expected to launch in 2002. Another product is Memantine, the leading treatment for Alzheimer's in Germany, which is in phase three clinical trials in the U.S. With its focused, low-cost approach to drug development and the growing demand for outsourcing of latter-stage development, Forest's prospects look good.

Celexa is such a huge success that it contributes over 60 percent of the company's revenues. The licensing deal ends in 2004, which gives it a couple of good years yet, in which the drug will likely grow to an even larger market share. Escitalopram should mitigate the eventual loss of Celexa, though Forest could very well negotiate a new deal.

A more serious threat comes from the expiration of the patent on Prozac in August 2001. Forest's sales force will have to convince physicians that the second generation of Celexa is superior enough to generic Prozac to warrant the extra expense.

Financial Highlights

While the computer and telecom sectors were nose-diving from March 2000 to March 2001, Forest Labs stock gained 40.2 percent. Meanwhile, revenues climbed 35 percent, with EPS up 28 percent. Concerns over a possible FDA reversal on patent protection for Biovail's Tiazac drug, which Forest distributes, caused a sharp drop in Forest's share price in March 2001. But the stock quickly recovered, and by July had resumed an upwards trend, which should continue for the next few years.

Forest Laboratories, Inc. at a Glance

Fiscal Year-end: March

10-Year Return: 22.9%

	1997	1998	1999	2000	2001	10-Year Growth Average (%)	10-Year Growth Total (%)
Revenue (US$ mlns.)	280.7	427.1	546.3	872.8	1,174.5	22.7	388.6
Net Income (US$ mlns.)	-36.1	57.9	77.2	168.0	224.7	–	353.0
Earnings/ Share (US$)	-0.21	0.35	0.45	0.96	1.23	–	339.3
Dividend/ Share (US$)	–	–	–	–	–	–	–
Price/ Earnings	-33.6 - -59.8	22.9 - 54.3	35.6 - 65.4	21.5 - 45.4	30.4 - 58.6	–	–

Table data courtesy of Canadian Shareowner   www.shareowner.com

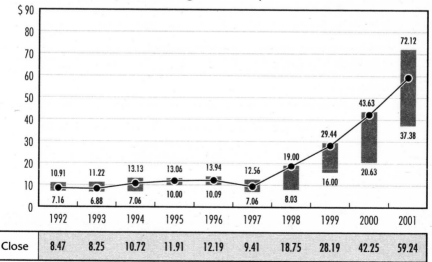

Stock Growth (Fiscal Year High-Low-Close)

	1992	1993	1994	1995	1996	1997	1998	1999	2000	2001
Close	8.47	8.25	10.72	11.91	12.19	9.41	18.75	28.19	42.25	59.24

PFIZER INC.

235 East 42nd Street
New York, NY 10017-5755

Tel: (212) 573-2323
www.pfizer.com
Symbol: PFE (NYSE)

Employees: 90,000
Founded: 1849
Listed: 1942

Chairperson, President, and CEO: Henry A. McKinnell

Share Price Growth	★ ★ ★ ★ ★
Revenue Growth	★ ★ ★
EPS Growth	★ ★ ★
PFE	**11**

About the Company

Pfizer is the largest and most profitable pharmaceutical company and third-largest company by market cap in America. Most people are familiar with it as the company that gave us Viagra, but it is much more than that.

Founded in 1849 by two immigrant cousins, Charles Pfizer and Charles Erhart, Pfizer started out as a chemical company. Early products were medicinal—an anti-parasitic, camphor, iodine, and borax, among others. In 1880 it found the product that would become its mainstay and source of growth for over 50 years: citric acid. A lemon shortage in World War I led to the discovery of how to make citric acid artificially by fermenting sugar. This was later refined into a deep-tank fermentation process using molasses. The stage was set for what was to become Pfizer's first major breakthrough in pharmaceuticals.

Alexander Fleming's discovery of penicillin in 1928 had gone undeveloped because of the inability to mass-produce it. But 10 years later, scientists at Oxford went to the U.S. to solve the production problem, and Pfizer successfully applied deep-tank fermentation to the task in 1944. Although 19 other companies were authorized to make penicillin, none could match Pfizer's production levels, and it supplied 90 percent of the penicillin used on the front lines for the rest of World War II.

Following the war, Pfizer set out to discover other antibiotics. Terramycin, the first proprietary product developed by Pfizer scientists, hit the market in 1950. This marked the transition from chemical company to drug company, and the rest, as they say, is history.

Today Pfizer manufactures dozens of drugs, eight of which generate over a billion dollars a year each in sales. The company also has a veterinary medicine division and an extensive Global Research and Development Division which had a budget approaching US$5 billion for 2001.

In June 2000, Pfizer acquired Warner Lambert, one of the world's leading patent medicine and consumer products manufacturers, with leading brands such as Listerine, Benadryl, Sudafed, Visine, BenGay, and Schick in its stable.

Opportunities and Challenges

Pfizer is in the forefront of pharmaceutical research, operating three research campuses in the U.S. as well as one each in France, Britain, and Japan. There are also numerous satellite research centres worldwide, in addition to strategic alliances with more than 250 partners in academia and industry.

How important is such research? How much impact can a successful new product have on the bottom line? Pfizer started research on fluconazole in 1970. It was introduced commercially as Diflucan in 1990 and is today the world's leading antifungal treatment. The late '70s saw work begin on amplodipine. Commercialized in 1992 as Norvasc, it is the world's leading antihypertensive and fourth best-selling drug in the world.

And let's not forget Viagra! Pfizer spent US$2.5 billion developing the drug. Today it generates over US$1.25 billion a year in sales.

Pfizer's biggest challenge currently is the successful integration of Warner Lambert into its operations. Although cost-saving synergies have already been realized, sales for the division declined 4 percent in the quarter to March 31, 2001. However, this quarter saw a 34 percent growth in net income and successful realization of cost-saving synergies in the Warner Lambert integration. The company believes new management, productivity improvements, and divestiture of non-core products will improve the division's bottom line. The second quarter saw sales up 10 percent over the previous year and diluted earnings per share up 59 percent.

Financial Highlights

Although Pfizer's stock has traded in a US$35–US$45 range for two and half years as of mid-2001, continuing growth in revenues and earnings should see the stock advancing in the future. This is a good long-term buy.

Pfizer Inc. at a Glance

Fiscal Year-end: December
10-Year Return: 26.3%

	1996	1997	1998	1999	2000	10-Year Growth Average (%)	10-Year Growth Total (%)
Revenue (US$ mlns.)	11,306.0	12,504.0	13,544.0	16,204.0	29,574.0	19.2	325.5
Net Income (US$ mlns.)	1,941.5	2,213.0	2,439.1	3,372.2	6,575.0	26.7	626.6
Earnings/ Share (US$)	0.50	0.57	0.62	0.87	1.03	19.0	368.2
Dividend/ Share (US$)	0.20	0.23	0.25	0.31	0.36	14.2	227.3
Price/ Earnings	20.1 - 30.4	23.6 - 46.8	38.2 - 69.3	36.3 - 57.5	29.1 - 47.8	–	–

Table data courtesy of Canadian Shareowner www.shareowner.com

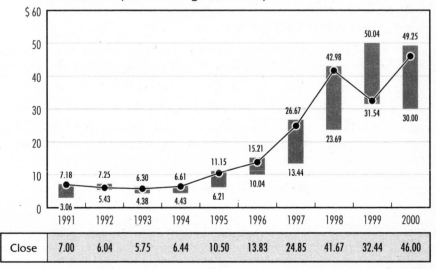

Stock Growth (Fiscal Year High-Low-Close)

Close	7.00	6.04	5.75	6.44	10.50	13.83	24.85	41.67	32.44	46.00

ARTHROCARE CORPORATION

595 North Pastoria Ave.
Sunnyvale, CA 94086-2916

Tel: (408) 736-0224   Employees: 272
Fax: (408) 736-0226   Founded: 1993
www.arthrocare.com   Listed: 1996
Symbol: ARTC (NASDAQ)

President and CEO: Michael Baker

Share Price Growth	★ ★ ★
Revenue Growth	★ ★ ★ ★ ★
EPS Growth	★ ★
ARTC	**10**

About the Company

Sometimes you go looking for one thing and find something else completely. Such was the case with ArthroCare, a surgical supply company in Sunnyvale, Cal. The company was set up to develop new tools for cardiovascular surgery, but the company's founders made an interesting discovery. Electrical impulses behaved differently when sent through a conductive solution than in the non-conductive environment used by traditional electro-surgical tools.

The old method of electro-surgical tissue removal involved heating tissue to temperatures approaching 400°C, causing it to literally explode or vaporize. This often caused heat damage to surrounding tissue. The new method used ionized plasma to disintegrate targeted tissue electrochemically. This discovery was refined and patented, and the technology named Coblation, a contraction of "cool ablation" (ablation is the technical term for surgical tissue removal). Coblation was found to be particularly useful for surgery on joints, or arthroscopic surgery, hence the company name.

In March 1995, the FDA cleared the company to market its arthroscopic system, and first products were shipped in August that year. The company now has 20 U.S. and 16 international patents on its system and has developed other uses for it. These include spinal surgery, cosmetic surgery, and ear, nose, and throat (ENT) surgery (or otorhinolaryngology, since we're showing off our vocabulary today. Sort of rolls right off the tongue, doesn't it?).

ArthroCare was the 13th fastest-growing company in America, according to the Deloitte & Touche Fast 500 for 2000.

Opportunities and Challenges

The company believes that Coblation can replace the multiple tools traditionally used in soft-tissue surgery with one handy multi-purpose system. The Coblation process is sold as a controller unit with attachable and disposable tools designed for specific purposes.

ArthroCare is continually exploring new avenues of development, introducing a specialized tool for delicate knee surgery and another for head, neck, and ENT surgery in the first quarter of 2001. The company is currently working with Boston Scientific to develop Coblation surgical tools for myocardial revascularization, a promising new treatment for heart disease.

ArthroCare markets Coblation through a network of distributors worldwide and has licensed Ethicon, a division of Johnson & Johnson, to use the technology for arthroscopy and gynecology.

ArthroCare has a fascinating and unique product with tremendous potential. Its biggest challenges are to continue developing new uses for the technology and to market it effectively. For the first quarter to March 31, 2001, ArthroCare's revenues increased 17.9 percent, though earnings were flat due to taxes. New product divisions, ENT and spinal, did particularly well.

Financial Highlights

ArthroCare had losses for its first three years as a public company. However, we allowed this exception to our screening criteria because the progression has been from declining losses to increasing profits, and for a young medical services company, this is not unusual. And its EPS more than doubled in 2000. After surging to over US$79 during the technology explosion in 2000, ArthroCare dropped below US$12 in March 2001. Since then the stock has been charting a steady upwards trend as investors learn about its story and prospects.

ArthroCare Corporation at a Glance

Fiscal Year-end: December

5-Year Return: 14.1%

	1996	1997	1998	1999	2000	6-Year Growth Average (%)	Total (%)
Revenue (US$ mlns.)	6.0	12.8	27.9	48.7	67.6	601.3	33,700.0
Net Income (US$ mlns.)	-7.7	-7.7	-2.1	5.5	15.8	–	–
Earnings/ Share (US$)	-0.47	-0.44	-0.12	0.27	0.68	–	–
Dividend/ Share (US$)	–	–	–	–	–	–	–
Price/ Earnings	-6.1 - -28.2	-6 - -16.8	-42.4 - -95.8	23.6 - 148.1	18 - 116.5	–	–

Table data courtesy of **Canadian Shareowner**   **www.shareowner.com**

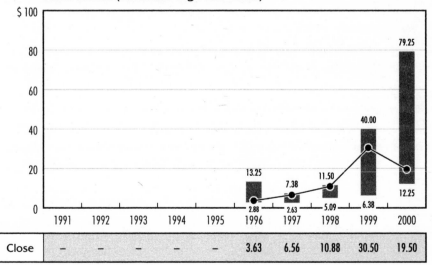

Stock Growth (Fiscal Year High-Low-Close)

MDS INC.

100 International Blvd.
Toronto, ON M9W 6J6

Tel: (416) 675-7661   Employees: 10,376
Fax: (416) 675-0688   Founded: 1969
www.mdsintl.com   Listed: 1973
Symbol: MDS (TSE) (Also MDZ-NYSE)

Chairperson: Wilfred G. Lewitt
President and CEO: John A. Rogers

Share Price Growth	★ ★ ★ ★ ★
Revenue Growth	★ ★ ★
EPS Growth	★ ★
MDS	**10**

About the Company

MDS Inc. is an international health and life sciences company employing over 10,000 people in over 20 countries besides Canada and the U.S. The health side of the business provides products and services to the health care industry, such as diagnostic services, managing hospital laboratories as joint ventures, distribution of medical supplies, distribution of emergency medical products, and manufacture of anesthesia equipment for dental and veterinary use.

On the life sciences side, MDS is involved in providing technology and services to manufacturers of medical products. This includes contract research for pharmaceutical and biotechnology companies, sterilization services, and the manufacture of specialized analytical instruments, nuclear isotopes for use in diagnostic imaging (MDS is the world's leading supplier of radioisotopes), and products and systems for radiation therapy. MDS's newest venture, launched in 2000, is proteomics research, the study of protein structures for the development of diagnostic tests and new drugs.

In the 30 years of its existence, MDS has grown from offering laboratory services in Canada into a world leader in medical supplies and services with over 60 percent of its business outside the country.

Opportunities and Challenges

MDS's proprietary AutoLab testing system has increased its efficiency and been a strong element in forging joint ventures to manage hospital laboratories on a contract basis. There are over 8,000 hospital-based laboratories in the U.S., providing 56 percent of all the diagnostic work done. AutoLab gives MDS the leverage to develop joint ventures in this US$20 billion market—the company has barely scratched the surface.

The new Proteomics Division is a bold venture into a field in its infancy. MDS's specialized spectrometry instrumentation, among other things, has excited joint venture partners such as the research department of Mt. Sinai Hospital in Toronto. Like the human genome project, proteomics may shed new light on the nature of disease and potential cures.

The year 2000 was pivotal for MDS, with shares being listed on the NYSE, new debt and equity financing, and the launch of MDS Proteomics, its largest R&D initiative ever. The half-billion-dollar acquisition of Phoenix International Life Sciences makes MDS the third-largest contract research organization in the world. The challenge now is to move ahead and shoot for number one as well as to maintain its leadership position in diagnostics and radiation therapy.

Financial Highlights

Since hitting a peak of $32 in September 2000, MDS stock has taken a beating, falling steadily to almost $16 in June 2001. Disappointing earnings were the primary culprit. Continuing issues with the integration of Phoenix International Life Sciences coupled with the company's substantial investment in its proteomics effort contributed to the lower numbers. But sales are up significantly, and the price-to-earnings ratio has been pushed to the low end of the usual range for MDS, making it a value buy.

MDS Inc. at a Glance

Fiscal Year-end: October

10-Year Return: 18.6%

	1996	1997	1998	1999	2000	10-Year Growth Average (%)	Total (%)
Revenue ($ mlns.)	818.9	930.0	1,001.5	1,191.7	1,444.9	18.4	334.9
Net Income ($ mlns.)	51.1	64.9	71.8	85.6	89.6	18.8	348.0
Earnings/ Share ($)	0.47	0.58	0.64	0.74	0.70	15.1	233.3
Dividend/ Share ($)	0.05	0.06	0.06	0.07	0.12	18.5	300.0
Price/ Earnings	10.5 - 20.5	16.1 - 30.8	18.8 - 27	18.6 - 23.5	18.8 - 46.3	–	–

Table data courtesy of Canadian Shareowner   www.shareowner.com

Stock Growth (Fiscal Year High-Low-Close)

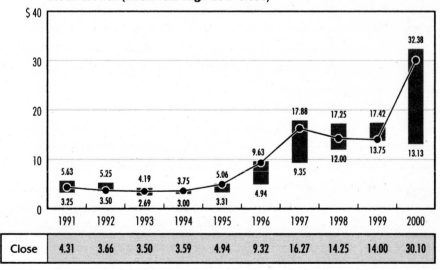

Close	4.31	3.66	3.50	3.59	4.94	9.32	16.27	14.25	14.00	30.10

MERCK & COMPANY, INC.

One Merck Drive, P.O. Box 100
Whitehouse Station, NJ 08889-0100

Tel: 1-800-613-2104   Employees: 62,000
www.merck.com   Founded: 1889
Symbol: MRK (NYSE)   Listed: 1946

Chairperson, President, and CEO: Raymond V. Gilmartin

Share Price Growth	★ ★ ★ ★
Revenue Growth	★ ★ ★
EPS Growth	★ ★
MRK	9

About the Company

Merck is a global pharmaceutical company with nine research and 30 manufacturing facilities serving people in approximately 200 countries worldwide. Its Canadian subsidiary, Merck Frosst Canada, operates the world-class Merck Frosst Centre for Therapeutic Research in Montreal. This is the largest private biomedical research facility in Canada, employing over 300 scientists and representing over 10 percent of the R&D budget for Canada's entire pharmaceutical industry.

With a research budget of close to US$3 billion annually, Merck has pioneered many medical advances in a number of fields, including atherosclerosis, hypertension, heart failure, anti-inflammatories, osteoporosis, and antibiotics. Research-driven new products accounted for 28 percent of sales in 1999. The company also has a veterinary medicine division.

Products include several billion-dollar annual sellers such as Zocor, used to reduce cholesterol levels, which sells around US$4.5 billion annually, Cozaar for high blood pressure, and Fosamax for osteoporosis.

Merck's largest revenue generator is Merck-Medco Managed Care, which accounted for half of the company's US$40 billion of sales in 2000. Merck-Medco offers pharmaceutical benefit management programs to provide affordable medicines to members of corporate, union, insurance company, and government health benefit plans. Individuals can subscribe online through the company's subsidiary, PAID Prescriptions. Merck-Medco serves 65 million Americans and operates the world's largest online pharmacy.

Merck is also a medical information company, publishing some of the largest reference works for doctors: *The Merck Index*, *The Merck Manual of Diagnosis and Therapy*, and *The Merck Manual of Geriatrics*. The Merck Manual is the most widely used medical text in the world, and since 1955, the *Merck Veterinary Manual* has been the standard reference for vets.

Sales have grown by better than 18 percent annually for the last 10 years, and grew 22.5 percent in 1999 and 23.4 percent in 2000, with annual growth increasing every year since 1995. Earnings per share have grown every year for the last 10, as have dividends.

Opportunities and Challenges

With 7,800 employees engaged in research at nine facilities in the U.S., Canada, Britain, Spain, Italy, France, and Japan, Merck is well positioned to continue developing new and profitable medications. Its focus has been varied and includes asthma, arthritis, cancer, diabetes, cardiovascular disease, osteoporosis, and immunology.

However, Merck-Medco has been an increasingly important source of growth for Merck. In 1998, it accounted for 43.1 percent of sales. That grew to 46.6 percent in 1999 and 49.9 percent in 2000. As health care costs increase and insurers and government agencies seek to reduce them, Merck-Medco's goal of being "the most influential force in controlling health care costs and supporting improved patient care through the appropriate use of pharmaceuticals" places the company in the right place and the right time for continued growth.

A solid first quarter to March 31, 2001 showed revenues up 28 percent over the year before and EPS up 13 percent. Despite modestly lowered expectations going into the second quarter, continued growth should propel the stock out of its trading range to the upside within the next year.

Financial Highlights

Merck stock rose steadily from 1996 through the end of 1999, when it started trading in a wide range between US$60 and US$90 for two years. It hit a new high of US$96 in December 2000 before falling back steadily to the US$60 level in July 2001, despite growing revenues and earnings. The pace of growth slowed, partly because of adverse currency exchange rates. The fundamentals of the company remain strong, and prices below US$90 represent a real bargain for the investor.

Merck & Company, Inc. at a Glance

Fiscal Year-end: December
10-Year Return: 16.5%

	1996	1997	1998	1999	2000	10-Year Growth Average (%)	10-Year Growth Total (%)
Revenue (US$ mlns.)	19,828.7	23,636.9	26,898.2	32,714.0	40,363.2	19.1	369.2
Net Income (US$ mlns.)	3,881.3	4,617.8	5,236.7	5,891.3	6,821.7	13.9	221.5
Earnings/ Share (US$)	1.57	1.87	2.15	2.45	2.90	14.0	222.2
Dividend/ Share (US$)	0.74	0.87	0.99	1.12	1.26	13.6	215.0
Price/ Earnings	18 - 26.8	20.9 - 28.9	23.6 - 37.6	24.9 - 35.7	17.9 - 33.3	–	–

Table data courtesy of **Canadian Shareowner**   **www.shareowner.com**

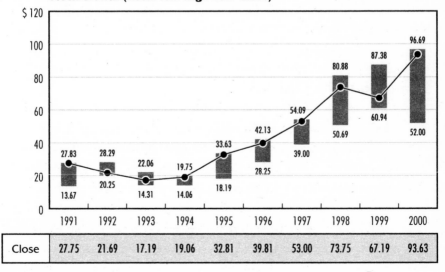

Stock Growth (Fiscal Year High-Low-Close)

| Close | 27.75 | 21.69 | 17.19 | 19.06 | 32.81 | 39.81 | 53.00 | 73.75 | 67.19 | 93.63 |

CANADIAN MEDICAL LABORATORIES LTD.

6560 Kennedy Road
Mississauga, ON L5T 2X4

Tel: (905) 565-0043
Fax: (905) 565-1776
www.canmedlab.com
Symbol: CLC (TSE)

Employees: 1,400
Founded: 1971
Listed: 1996

Chairperson, President, and CEO: John D. Mull, MD
CFO: Paul J. Bristow

Share Price Growth	★ ★
Revenue Growth	★ ★
EPS Growth	★ ★
CLC	6

About the Company

Founded by a doctor to serve doctors, Canadian Medical Laboratories has grown from modest beginnings to become the largest medical testing laboratory business in Ontario, serving 20,000 to 30,000 patients daily through over 150 facilities. Its laboratory stable includes wholly owned subsidiaries CyberMedix Inc., Fort Frances Inc., and LabCare Inc. They offer a complete range of testing services, including histology, hematology, biochemistry, cytology, and microbiology. Combined, CML's lab facilities have 33 percent of the Ontario market.

Since going public in 1996, the company has moved into the clinical research business. The lucrative laboratory business has financed this expansion, which promises to generate even more growth for the company. The clinical research business consists of three wholly owned subsidiaries. Novoquest Research is the U.S. arm, which aims to grow through aggressive acquisition. Pharma Medica Research provides research for the pharmacokinetic (medical devices) field as well as bio-analytical services. To promote these research services, the company formed the third branch—the Academic Network for Clinical Research Inc. ANCR, through a corporate partnership with the Association of Professors of Medicine, manages and markets clinical trial services at 125 medical schools in the U.S.

In 2000, CML launched a new subsidiary, Cipher Pharmaceuticals, to develop innovative new drugs. It already has two licensing agreements with Galephar Pharmaceutical Research to develop a lipid-lowering product and a controlled-release version of Galephar's pain-killer Tramadol. Cipher launched its first investigational new drug application for the lipid-lowering drug in late June 2001.

Canadian Medical Labs has more than tripled annual revenues since 1996. It is consistently profitable, so much so that it actually knocked down $36 million of its long-term debt in fiscal 2000.

Opportunities and Challenges

The laboratory testing business forms a solid and profitable core foundation for the company and gives it the financial clout to pursue its expansion into the research field, which is still developing. The research market, which currently generates only around 15 to 20 percent of CML's revenues, promises to be the generator of growth in the future.

The clinical research market in the U.S. is estimated at US$3.5 billion a year, but it is highly fragmented, with no single company capturing more than 1 percent of the market. CML is working to consolidate its position through acquisition of some of the many players. In fiscal 2000 it acquired Boca Raton Medical Research in Florida, as well as Hartford Research Group, with facilities in Ohio and Kentucky. CML also owns a majority interest in Summit Research, which has operations in four states focused on central nervous system disorders.

The challenge for Canadian Medical Labs is to integrate its research acquisitions into a market-dominating whole. As of this writing, the research arm of the company was losing money, although the losses are shrinking. The company must successfully manage growth of its money-losing division without tapping out its profitable lab testing business. Fortunately, the profits of the one division are very large compared to the losses of the other, by better than 18 to 1.

Revenues were flat for the quarter ended March 31, 2001, with earnings down 20.9 percent. This was due to softer-than-expected research revenue. But a backlog of studies and introduction of cost-cutting initiatives should turn things around. There's also the prospect of growing the highly successful lab testing business, possibly into other provinces.

Financial Highlights

Canadian Medical's stock has been trading in a broad range from $14 to $20 from January 2000 through July 2001. With solid revenue growth averaging 58.8 percent a year and earnings growth averaging 66.4 percent, the stock started testing its 52-week highs in mid-2001. Continued growth, if it can be achieved, should be reflected in the stock price over the next few years.

Canadian Medical Laboratories Ltd. at a Glance

Fiscal Year-end: September

3-Year Return: 34.8%

	1996	1997	1998	1999	2000	5-Year Growth Average (%)	5-Year Growth Total (%)
Revenue ($ mlns.)	53.9	71.0	74.5	130.4	186.0	38.6	245.1
Net Income ($ mlns.)	6.2	7.1	11.3	23.5	32.8	55.3	429.7
Earnings/ Share ($)	–	0.46	0.58	1.16	1.54	53.0	234.8
Dividend/ Share ($)	–	–	–	–	–	–	–
Price/ Earnings	–	9.8 - 15.5	10.3 - 15.1	4.8 - 21.2	9.1 - 15.6	–	–

Table data courtesy of Canadian Shareowner   www.shareowner.com

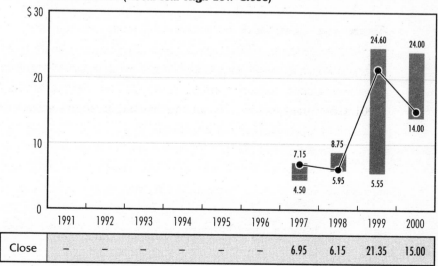

Stock Growth (Fiscal Year High-Low-Close)

	1991	1992	1993	1994	1995	1996	1997	1998	1999	2000
Close	–	–	–	–	–	–	6.95	6.15	21.35	15.00

Note: Data for the years 1996–97 from company reports. EPS growth figures based on four years.

ZENON ENVIRONMENTAL INC.

3239 Dundas Street West
Oakville, ON L6M 4B2

Tel: (905) 465-3030
Fax: (905) 465-3050
www.zenonenv.com
Symbol: ZEN (TSE)

Employees: 501
Founded: 1980
Listed: 1992

Chairperson and CEO: Andrew Benedek

Share Price Growth	★ ★
Revenue Growth	★ ★
EPS Growth	0
ZEN	**4**

About the Company

We turn on the tap and out it comes—clean, fresh water. We flush the toilet and there it goes—not so clean, not so fresh water. We tend to take these things for granted. But water, whether it's coming or going, needs to be treated, and Zenon Environmental is one of the leading companies developing and marketing both water purification and waste-water treatment plants.

Zenon's patented ZeeWeed hollow-fibre membrane technology works by reverse osmosis to separate particulates and contaminants from water. The fibres draw in water under slight suction to produce clear, clean drinking water. Fibre pores vary to as little as 0.01 microns in size, small enough to filter out infectious agents such as crypto-sporidium and giardia.

The ZeeWeed modules can be adapted to existing treatment facilities, allowing for low-cost retrofitting. But many clients have contracted for complete filtration systems from scratch, including the Olivenhain Municipal Water District in Southern California, which completed the largest ultra-filtration water treatment plant in North America in January 2001 using Zenon technology.

Zenon is international in scope, with operations in Europe, the Middle East, Latin America, and Asia. It also makes shipboard filtration systems for cruise ships, the merchant marine, and navies.

Opportunities and Challenges

Tragedy struck the town of Walkerton, Ont., in May 2000 when E. coli infected the water supply: seven people died and many more became seriously ill. The scandal led to a government inquiry and the establishment of Operation Clean Water, a concerted effort to introduce universal water quality standards in the province.

Walkerton is not an isolated incident. Exactly a year later, three people were reported killed by water-borne bacteria in North Battleford, Saskatchewan. These tragedies have highlighted the problem of aging and inferior infrastructure and the need for remediation.

The town of Collingwood built the first ZeeWeed plant in 1996, and by the end of 2000 there were 22 completed or under design in the province. Ninety percent of Ontario's drinking-water facilities turned to Zenon membrane technology in 2000, including Walkerton.

Although there was a lull in the market in the first half of 2000, Zenon invested heavily in new manufacturing capacity and product development, opening a new head office and assembly plant in June and a major extension to the manufacturing plant in November. The company can now handle over $200 million in sales.

Zenon is poised to be a major player, as municipalities around North America and the world re-evaluate their drinking-water and wastewater treatment facilities.

Zenon had a backlog of $72 million at the end of 2000, and despite expanded facilities, Zenon's biggest challenge may well be keeping up with demand. The company's checkered EPS record does not meet the criteria we established for this book, but we have made an exception because of the particular nature of Zenon's business and its strong prospects for the future.

Results for the first quarter to March 31, 2001 showed revenues up 46.9 percent and a loss of a penny a share, down from a loss of $0.07 the year before.

Financial Highlights

Although Zenon is one of the few companies we're covering that showed a loss in 2000, it is poised for strong recovery and earnings growth because of its unique business. When the North Battleford situation became public in May 2001, the stock took a strong leap forward, from $8.00 to $15.50 by July. With an impressive backlog and growing demand, the future for Zenon looks bright.

Zenon Environmental Inc. at a Glance

Fiscal Year-end: December

8-Year Return: 13.1%

	1996	1997	1998	1999	2000	9-Year Growth Average (%)	9-Year Growth Total (%)
Revenue ($ mlns.)	53.2	58.4	77.2	98.8	84.5	16.5	168.3
Net Income ($ mlns.)	0.4	2.2	4.8	2.7	-2.8	–	-86.7
Earnings/ Share ($)	0.02	0.12	0.22	0.12	-0.12	–	-7.7
Dividend/ Share ($)	–	–	–	–	–	–	–
Price/ Earnings	65 - 247.5	34.4 - 67.9	30.7 - 65.6	62.5 - 171.9	-46.7 - -104.2	–	–

Table data courtesy of Canadian Shareowner www.shareowner.com

Stock Growth (Fiscal Year High-Low-Close)

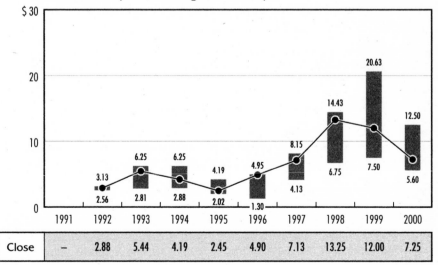

Close	–	2.88	5.44	4.19	2.45	4.90	7.13	13.25	12.00	7.25

ENERGY

Calpine Corporation
Pason Systems Inc.
Canadian Hydro Developers, Inc.
Trican Well Service Ltd.

CALPINE CORPORATION

50 West San Fernando Street
San Jose, CA 95113

Tel: (408) 995-5115   Employees: 1,000
Fax: (408) 995-0505   Founded: 1984
www.calpine.com   Listed: 1996
Symbol: CPN (NYSE) (Also CPX-TSE)

President and CEO: Pete Cartwright

Share Price Growth	★ ★ ★ ★ ★
Revenue Growth	★ ★ ★ ★ ★
EPS Growth	★ ★ ★ ★ ★
CPX	**15**

About the Company

Calpine Corporation is the fastest-growing independent producer of electricity in the U.S. and the world's largest provider of power from geothermal sources.

Founded in 1984 by its visionary leader, Pete Cartwright, Calpine focuses on producing electricity using new and environmentally friendly technologies. While the established power companies continue to struggle along with outdated, inefficient coal-fired plants, Calpine is building fuel-efficient natural gas plants as well as developing geothermal energy.

Coal-fired plants are cheaper to build and operate than natural gas plants, and better catalytic converters and emission treatment have enabled the industry to cope with potential pollution problems. However, coal-fired plants take six years to build, compared to just 30 months for a gas-powered plant, which works in Calpine's favour because of the pace of new demand.

Calpine's slogan is "Repowering America," and its goal is no less than to become the largest and most profitable power company in America.

Opportunities and Challenges

The electricity needs of the U.S. are growing at over 3 percent a year. Much of that demand is being driven by the communications revolution. Computers, embedded chips, servers—all are consuming power, sometimes 24 hours a day. Computers already consume 13 percent of the power produced in the U.S., and that is expected to increase to 50 percent in the next decade. The U.S. has been experiencing periodic power shortages as supply fails to keep pace with demand.

Deregulation has allowed Calpine to enter new markets with efficient new plants and underprice its competitors. It now operates 50 plants in over 20 states and Alberta, and plans to have 100 in operation by 2005.

The company has grown revenues from US$97.5 million in 1994 to US$2,258.2 million in 2000, with annual growth rates accelerating from 64.6 percent to 178.4 percent over the period. The company has been profitable since 1994, with earnings per share growing almost as fast as revenues.

How much room does that leave it to grow? The company is still only a fraction the size of such giants as Duke Energy (US$25 billion in revenues). Power generation is, in fact, the third-largest industry in North America, after health care and the automotive industry.

The deregulation of power in California was a crazy quilt of illogic, in which the market was deregulated at the wholesale level, but not at the retail level. This means that companies supplying power directly to consumers, such as Pacific Gas and Electric, have experienced tough financial problems as they buy increasingly expensive electricity on the spot market but are not allowed to pass on these costs to consumers. Hence Calpine's number-one problem—collecting from debtors such as PG&E.

The price of natural gas has skyrocketed in recent years, and this also poses a challenge to Calpine's bottom line. The company is vertically integrating by buying up natural gas companies to assure itself continuous supply. The April 2001 merger with Canada's Encal Energy is a case in point. This acquisition resulted in exchangeable shares of Calpine trading on the Toronto Stock Exchange.

Financial Highlights

Calpine is growing at a torrid pace, and is one of 16 companies to get a full 15-star rating in this book. Revenues have been accelerating year to year as have earnings. The stock price, however, came under pressure in the first half of 2001 due to concerns over the solvency of Calpine's debtors. In July 2001, the California bankruptcy courts effectively gave Calpine preferred creditor status with PG&E in a five-year deal.

Calpine Corporation at a Glance

Fiscal Year-end: December

4-Year Return: 109.4%

	1996	1997	1998	1999	2000	7-Year Growth Average (%)	7-Year Growth Total (%)
Revenue (US$ mlns.)	208.0	260.5	530.7	811.1	2,258.2	75.5	2,216.1
Net Income (US$ mlns.)	18.7	34.7	46.3	96.2	324.7	104.6	4,746.3
Earnings/ Share (US$)	0.16	0.21	0.27	0.43	1.16	69.6	1,557.1
Dividend/ Share (US$)	–	–	–	–	–	–	–
Price/ Earnings	12.5 - 15.6	7.4 - 13.7	5.9 - 12.8	7.3 - 38.1	13.9 - 45.7	–	–

Table data courtesy of Canadian Shareowner   www.shareowner.com

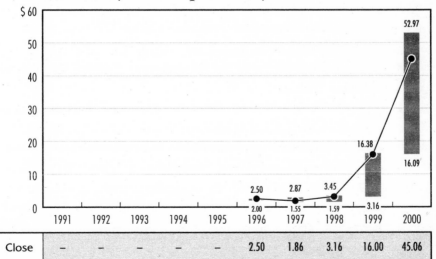

Stock Growth (Fiscal Year High-Low-Close)

Close	–	–	–	–	–	2.50	1.86	3.16	16.00	45.06

PASON SYSTEMS INC.

6130-3rd Street S.E.
Calgary, AB T2H 1K4

Tel: (403) 301-3400
Fax: (403) 301-3499
www.pason.com
Symbol: PSI (TSE)

Employees: 180
Founded: 1992
Listed: 1996

Chairperson and President: Jim Hill

Share Price Growth	★ ★
Revenue Growth	★ ★ ★ ★ ★
EPS Growth	★ ★ ★ ★
PSI	**11**

About the Company

Pason Systems is bringing the digital age to the oil patch. The company provides a variety of electronic monitoring services at the wellhead that allow head offices to follow activity at drilling sites.

Pason's Penless Electronic Drilling Recorder (EDR) records, stores, and reports drilling parameters and events to assist drillers in monitoring and planning their activities. Each rig is networked to share drilling data with geology and engineering personnel in real time.

The Pit Bull PVT (Pit Volume Totalizer) enhances drilling safety by giving early warning of high-pressure hydrocarbon inflow "kicks." It's considered functional, reliable, and easy to use.

Pason technology also includes LPLOT, its proprietary mudlogging software. (Mud is a colloidal suspension of clay and chemical additives in water that is circulated through a wellbore during drilling.) And Pason's Internet Data Hub lets home office management monitor drilling remotely.

All this stuff used to be done with pen and paper and oral reports by telephone. But, as Dundee Securities put it in a May 2001 research report, "Pason is quietly and quickly bringing the management of drilling rigs into the 21st century."

Opportunities and Challenges

Pason has grown from annual revenues of just $500,000 in 1992 to $43.5 million in 2000. It has captured 82 percent of the Canadian market for EDRs, outfitting over 450 rigs. The company's next big push is the U.S. market, where 50 percent of rigs are outfitted with EDRs, a third of those Pason's. Pason systems were in place on over 200 rigs south of the border at the end of May 2001. The company expects to increase its market penetration to 350 rigs by the end of 2001.

Pason is constantly adding new products to its line, including the Electronic Choke System, designed to replace hydraulically operated wellhead valves, and the Total Gas System, which monitors natural gases entering the borehole. These products have barely dented Pason's revenues so far, but could contribute up to 20 percent in the future. The company is also working on an electronic oilfield accounting and payment system—another potentially strong revenue generator.

Because Pason's products are leased, they provide a constant revenue stream, rather than just a one-shot sale. The first quarter of 2001 to March 31 showed a 59.4 percent increase in revenues and an 81 percent increase in earnings per share over the same period in 2000.

President and chairperson Jim Hill owns 33 percent of the company, with insiders holding a further 15 percent. That spells a strong commitment to the success of the company.

Two challenges face Pason going forward. First is market saturation, since its products are already used on over 80 percent of Canadian rigs. New product development and increased inroads into the U.S.

market are keys to future growth. The international arena offers further opportunities that the company has not yet explored.

The second challenge is the oil industry itself. Pason's performance is tied to the industry, and while the industry is in expansion mode, this spells extremely good fortune for Pason. But if oil prices fall and exploration and development tail off, Pason's growth could be affected. The forecast as of May 2001 is for strong growth in drilling, but circumstances could change.

Financial Highlights

Pason stock has fluctuated to a certain extent with the oil industry. Since February 1999, however, Pason has been in a long upward trend with occasional flat or moderately declining periods. Revenues and earnings nearly doubled in 2000 as the oil industry found its legs again.

Pason Systems Inc. at a Glance

Fiscal Year-end: December

4-Year Return: 28.5%

	1996	1997	1998	1999	2000	5-Year Growth Average (%)	5-Year Growth Total (%)
Revenue ($ mlns.)	4.5	14.5	23.8	24.7	43.5	91.6	866.7
Net Income ($ mlns.)	0.9	4.1	4.9	4.1	8.1	113.2	800.0
Earnings/ Share ($)	0.07	0.26	0.28	0.23	0.47	91.4	571.4
Dividend/ Share ($)	–	–	–	–	–	–	–
Price/ Earnings	22.1 - 40.7	7.9 - 30.8	8.9 - 30.4	9.8 - 30	11.7 - 20.7	–	–

Table data courtesy of Canadian Shareowner   www.shareowner.com

Stock Growth (Fiscal Year High-Low-Close)

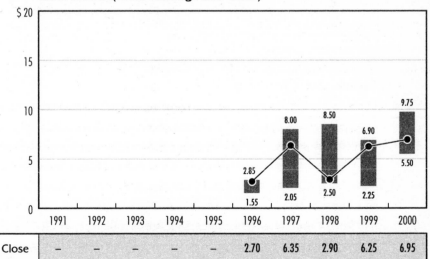

	1991	1992	1993	1994	1995	1996	1997	1998	1999	2000
Close	–	–	–	–	–	2.70	6.35	2.90	6.25	6.95

CANADIAN HYDRO DEVELOPERS, INC.

1324-17th Avenue S.W., Suite 500
Calgary, AB T2T 5S8

Tel: (403) 269-9379
Fax: (403) 244-7388
www.canhydro.com
Symbol: KHD (TSE)

Employees: 18
Founded: 1990
Listed: 1995

CEO: John D. Keating
President and COO: J. Ross Keating

Share Price Growth	★ ★ ★
Revenue Growth	★ ★ ★ ★ ★
EPS Growth	★ ★
KHD	**10**

About the Company

Founded in 1990, Canadian Hydro Developers' objective is to generate electricity in an environmentally friendly way. The company operates 11 power plants in Ontario, Alberta, and British Columbia: nine "run-of-river" hydro plants, one natural gas plant, and one wind plant. Five more hydro plants are under development in B.C., Alberta, and Ontario, as well as a biomass plant in Grande Prairie, Alta., that will burn wood waste from a nearby Canfor mill. Also in Alberta, the Drywood natural gas plant and the Cowley Ridge wind farm are being expanded.

Canadian Hydro has experienced a 35 percent annual growth in electricity generating capacity for the last five years, a figure it expects to ramp up to 50 percent over the next three. Its production capacity of 62.3 megawatts (as of March 2001) is expected to grow to 215 megawatts by the end of 2004.

In November 2000, the company offered power directly to the general public for the first time—previously it had fed power into the provincial grid or to business clients. Consumers in parts of Ontario and Alberta now have the choice of buying electricity certified as Ecologo emissions-free energy under Environment Canada's Environmental Choice program.

Opportunities and Challenges

It's estimated that demand for electricity in the U.S. is growing at 3 percent a year, yet supply is not keeping up. We've already seen rolling blackouts in California. Other jurisdictions, including New York, Louisiana, Illinois, and Texas, are also feeling the pinch. California even asked the U.S. Navy to hook up a few nuclear submarines to the grid to get it through the summer of 2001. (The Navy declined!) In Canada, the situation is similar. Low reservoir levels and the decommissioning of nuclear power plants have added to the strain.

With increasing deregulation of electricity generation, private companies such as Canadian Hydro Developers are filling the breach.

Can it compete with the big utilities? You bet! All of Canadian Hydro's power plants are less than 12 years old—new by industry standards. Half of them are less than five years old. All are state-of-the-art technology, requiring no staffing and low maintenance. However, low snowpacks have impacted the generating capacity of some of Canadian Hydro's plants in the past and may do so again in the future.

Canadian Hydro is also a founding member of the KEFI Exchange (see www.KEFI-Exchange.com), a system for exchanging pollution credits. Credits are a market-based greenhouse gas control mechanism that reward environmentally sound companies and penalize dirty producers (such as coal-powered plants). The idea of the KEFI Exchange is that utilities unable to meet mandated CO_2 emissions standards may purchase credits from companies that do meet them. As a low-emissions generator of electricity, Canadian Hydro Developers may have the opportunity to earn revenues from selling pollution credits to less clean companies. However, such revenues may not materialize at all, as President George W. Bush has indicated an antipathy towards the Kyoto Accord that mandates lower greenhouse gas emissions.

The main challenge for Canadian Hydro is to keep growing with demand. The company has had to resort to additional placements of stock warrants to raise capital in the last two years, which will ultimately lead to share dilution as the warrants are exercised. But the construction of new plants and increasing revenues should more than offset that.

A forward-hedging program has 75 percent of current production sold ahead for the next 12 years. This cuts into potential profits from an increasing spot price in electricity.

Financial Highlights

Canadian Hydro Developers was one of the top 10 performing stocks on the TSE in 2000, with a gain of 298.7 percent. This is not surprising considering the strong growth in revenues and earnings posted by the company. But the first half 2001 saw moderate earnings in spite of continued growth, with the stock price finding a range between $2.50 and $3.50. New projects coming onstream should propel the stock forward again in late 2001 and throughout 2002.

Canadian Hydro Developers, Inc. at a Glance

Fiscal Year-end: December

7-Year Return: 25.1%

	1996	1997	1998	1999	2000	7-Year Growth Average (%)	7-Year Growth Total (%)
Revenue ($ mlns.)	3.9	5.3	6.1	9.3	17.2	57.5	1,046.7
Net Income ($ mlns.)	0.2	0.5	0.4	1.3	2.8	–	–
Earnings/ Share ($)	0.02	0.03	0.01	0.05	0.10	–	–
Dividend/ Share ($)	–	–	–	–	–	–	–
Price/ Earnings	21.9 - 47.5	18.3 - 41.7	90 - 160	13 - 22	7.2 - 32	–	–

Table data courtesy of Canadian Shareowner   www.shareowner.com

Stock Growth (Fiscal Year High-Low-Close)

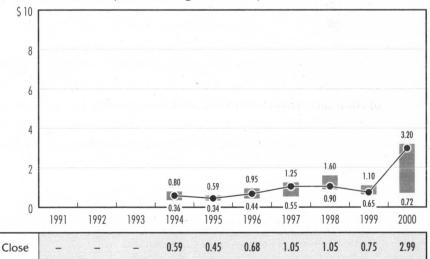

	1991	1992	1993	1994	1995	1996	1997	1998	1999	2000
Close	–	–	–	0.59	0.45	0.68	1.05	1.05	0.75	2.99

TRICAN WELL SERVICE LTD.

645-7th Avenue S.W., Suite 2900
Calgary, AB T2P 4G8

Tel: (403) 266-0202   Employees: 626
Fax: (403) 237-7716   Founded: 1979
www.trican.ca   Listed: 1996
Symbol: TCW (TSE)

President and CEO: Murray Cobbe

Share Price Growth		★ ★ ★
Revenue Growth		★ ★ ★
EPS Growth		★ ★ ★
TCW		**9**

About the Company

You might think that an oil services business is out of place in a book on science and technology stocks. And indeed, many of the services provided by Trican seem elementary—pumping, pouring cement, sticking tubing down a well. But the business does demand an understanding of geology and the application of specialized technology to attain results. For example:

- Cementing: Oil and gas wells need cementing treatments from a highly specialized apparatus during the drilling phase to support the production casing inside the wellbore.

- Coiled tubing: Thousands of feet of jointless steel pipe coiled on a reel is run into a well to allow the introduction of nitrogen, acids, and other materials to remove unwanted fluids or solids. This allows a well to remain in production while impurities are removed.
- Fracturing: Sometimes geological formations do not allow a smooth, steady flow of oil, so fluid is pumped into the cased well at high pressure to fracture the formation. A "proppant" is then injected into the fracture to prop it open.

Trican had a modest beginning in 1979—two pumping units and a bulk truck—and it continued to be modest until going public in 1996. Then, with new management, the company proceeded to expand. First it entered the cementing, coiled tubing, and nitrogen markets, followed by the acquisition of Superior Cementers. It continued to add new gear, including fracturing equipment, spending $61 million on equipment in its first three years as a public company.

In the fall of 2000, Trican opened a 6,000-square-foot research facility in Red Deer, Alta., the second-largest lab of its type in Western Canada. The company has a number of patents pending on proprietary systems it has developed, as well as patents for three new surfactant gelled fracturing fluids. It has also developed new lightweight "titanium" cements and a variety of specialized equipment. A redesigned liquid CO_2 blender and Canada's first "one-truck" fracturing unit give the company significant competitive advantages.

Today the pumping business makes up only half of the company's revenue. The rest comes from fracturing, nitrogen, and coiled tubing. Trican's revenues have grown over 350 percent since going public, and the stock has outperformed the TSE Oil and Gas index since the first quarter of 2000. Trican's stated goal is to become the dominant Canadian player in well services. Trican Well Services was added to the TSE 300 index in December 2000.

Opportunities and Challenges

The company has benefited greatly from the oil boom and grown steadily. In December 2000 it completed its acquisition of Canadian Oilfield Stimulation Services. Also in December 2000, Trican obtained the Canadian rights to the patented Polybore system. This process facilitates the repair of a wellbore, thereby extending its life. The company's primary business has been oil well services, but it is also pursuing new technology for the gas market.

Trican is another of the stocks that bucked the technology downturn, no doubt because it served a booming industry—oil. If and when the price of oil drops again, much of this business may dissipate. But Trican is diversifying, and the coiled tubing business is less prone to market fluctuations since it is used as much for well enhancement and life extension as for new drilling.

For the first quarter of 2001 to March 31, revenues jumped 79 percent over the same quarter the year before, while earnings per share leaped 149 percent.

Financial Highlights

Like our other oil well services company, Pason Systems, Trican's stock took a dip in 1998 while the oil industry languished from low prices. But since then, revenues, earnings, and the stock price have done very well indeed. Moderating oil prices and increasing inventory buildup took a hit on the company and other oil industry stocks in June 2001, a problem facing any company serving a commodity-based industry. Investors should keep a finger on the pulse of the oil market while holding industry stocks.

Trican Well Service Ltd. at a Glance

Fiscal Year-end: December

4-Year Return: 54.3%

	1996	1997	1998	1999	2000	4-Year Growth Average (%)	4-Year Growth Total (%)
Revenue ($ mlns.)	–	28.1	39.5	61.8	130.9	69.6	365.8
Net Income ($ mlns.)	–	2.2	1.8	4.9	14.8	117.4	572.7
Earnings/ Share ($)	–	0.23	0.15	0.34	0.88	83.6	282.6
Dividend/ Share ($)	–	–	–	–	–	–	–
Price/ Earnings	–	11.5 - 37	15 - 43.3	5 - 21.9	7.2 - 19.3	–	–

Table data courtesy of **Canadian Shareowner** **www.shareowner.com**

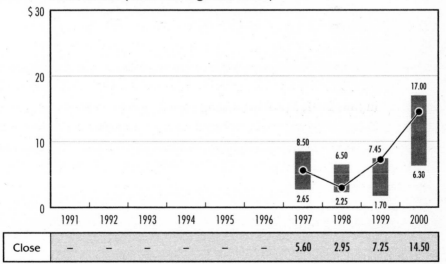

Stock Growth (Fiscal Year High-Low-Close)

	1991	1992	1993	1994	1995	1996	1997	1998	1999	2000
Close	–	–	–	–	–	–	5.60	2.95	7.25	14.50

INDUSTRY

Cree, Inc.
ATS Automation Tooling Systems Inc.
Magna International Inc.
Bombardier Inc.
Gennum Corporation
Silent Witness Enterprises Ltd.
BW Technologies Ltd.
DuPont Canada Inc.
CAE Inc.
Tesma International Inc.
Magellan Aerospace Corporation

CREE, INC.

4600 Silicon Drive
Durham, NC 27703

Tel: (919) 313-5300
Fax: (919) 313-5452
www.cree.com
Symbol: CREE (NASDAQ)

Employees: 680
Founded: 1987
Listed: 1993

Chairperson and CEO: F. Neal Hunter
President and COO: Charles M. Swoboda

Share Price Growth	★ ★ ★ ★ ★
Revenue Growth	★ ★ ★ ★ ★
EPS Growth	★ ★ ★ ★ ★
CREE	**15**

About the Company

If you've got a pocket calculator, or a clock with digital numbers, or an electronic display on the dashboard of your car, you're familiar with light-emitting diodes, or LEDs as they're usually called. Used in everything from cellular phones to giant electronic billboards, LEDs are made by dozens of companies. Cree is one of them, but it stands out because it chose to focus on a particular semiconductor compound—silicon carbide (SiC).

Cree is the world leader in the design and manufacturing of SiC-based electronic components. The optoelectronics field was plagued for a long time with the difficulty of developing an LED that emits blue light. SiC proved to be the solution, and Cree dominates the blue LED market through 73 U.S. and 45 foreign patents. To "own" a colour, and a primary colour at that, is very lucrative.

Cree also makes SiC wafers for university and corporate research facilities looking to develop new applications using the compound. Other applications in the works or in production include power-switching devices, blue and near-ultraviolet laser diodes, transistors, and ersatz gemstones. With the acquisition of Nitres Corporation in May 2000, the company has a solid presence in gallium nitride semiconductors as well.

In 2000, Cree was ranked as the 11th fastest-growing company in America by *Fortune* magazine.

Opportunities and Challenges

In May 2001 the company introduced a Megabright Blue LED twice as bright as the Ultrabright model launched in November 2000. Intensity has jumped tenfold in the last three years. This makes the product especially suitable for backlighting in PDAs, outdoor displays, contour lighting, and special effects lighting.

More interestingly, blue, combined with green and red, produces white light. A white LED would be 12 times more efficient and long-lasting than the ordinary incandescent light bulb. This could revolutionize the lighting industry. Cree is working to develop products for the commercial lighting market over the next few years.

Other Cree research projects also show tremendous commercial potential. Blue lasers, once commercialized, will effectively quadruple the storage capacity of DVDs and CD-ROMs, as well as improve the resolution of laser printers. And the company is developing SiC-based transistors that deliver five times the power of previous methods for radio frequency and microwave transmission applications. This could be a key ingredient in third-generation cellular and wireless telephone technology.

Although Cree has a 34 percent share of the worldwide LED market, it is not, in fact, the only player in the blue LED market. Nichia Corporation of Japan has developed blue LEDs based on gallium nitrides, and lawsuits have resulted. Cree won a suit filed against it by Nichia in Japan in May 2001, and nine days later Cree launched its own suit against Nichia in the U.S. The suit is based on gallium nitride patents acquired in the Nitres takeover and does not affect the company's hold on the SiC LED market. Cree is also developing chips that combine silicon carbide and gallium nitride to produce a superior product.

Financial Highlights

Cree's stock took a nice little swan dive in the technology debacle, falling from a high of US$101.00 in March 2000 to a low of US$12.21 at the market's nadir in early April 2001. Since then it has made a desultory climb back above the US$20 level as of mid-2001. Revenues and earnings continue to grow apace and, in more ways than one, the future looks bright.

Cree, Inc. at a Glance

Fiscal Year-end: June
8-Year Return: 36.8%

	1997	1998	1999	2000	2001	10-Year Growth Average (%)	10-Year Growth Total (%)
Revenue (US$ mlns.)	29.0	42.5	60.0	108.6	177.2	59.0	5,808.0
Net Income (US$ mlns.)	4.1	5.8	12.9	30.0	48.2	–	–
Earnings/ Share (US$)	0.08	0.11	0.23	0.43	0.64	–	–
Dividend/ Share (US$)	–	–	–	–	–	–	–
Price/ Earnings	25.8 - 49.6	26.7 - 67	11.4 - 86.1	27.3 - 234.9	19.1 - 123.3	–	–

Table data courtesy of ✓*Canadian Shareowner* **www.shareowner.com**

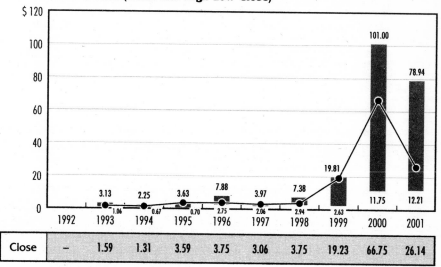

Stock Growth (Fiscal Year High-Low-Close)

| Close | – | 1.59 | 1.31 | 3.59 | 3.75 | 3.06 | 3.75 | 19.23 | 66.75 | 26.14 |

Note: Data for 2001 from company reports.

ATS AUTOMATION TOOLING SYSTEMS INC.

250 Royal Oak Road
Box 32100, Preston Centre
Cambridge, ON N3H 5M2

Tel: (519) 653-6500
Fax: (519) 653-6533
www.atsautomation.com
Symbol: ATA (TSE)

Employees: 3,400
Founded: 1978
Listed: 1993

Chairperson: L. G. Tapp
President and CEO: Klaus D. Woerner

Share Price Growth	★ ★ ★ ★ ★
Revenue Growth	★ ★ ★ ★ ★
EPS Growth	★ ★ ★ ★
ATA	**14**

About the Company

Word association—quickly now—what country do you associate with the following: Clean, efficient factories? Robotics? Automation? Chances are you answered Japan, the country we usually associate with technically advanced, automated factory assembly lines. But a Canadian company, ATS Automation Tooling, is a worldwide leader in developing automated solutions for industry.

After working for several years as a process engineer at Ford's Truck Division, Klaus Woerner founded ATS in 1978. The company designs and builds turn-key automated manufacturing systems, as well as manufacturing precision components for industry. Customers are generally multinational corporations.

ATS employs 3,400 people in 27 facilities across Canada, the U.S., Europe, and the Pacific Rim. This workforce is highly skilled: 44 percent are engineers and technical specialists, 21 percent are skilled tradespeople, and the remaining 38 percent are semi-skilled operators and administrators.

Among other things, the company has developed manufacturing solutions for the auto industry (it has been a preferred vendor for Ford since 1992), including assembly facilities for steering, suspension, drivetrain, braking, fuel, seating, windows, wipers, instrumentation, locks, and lighting systems. ATS is also one of the top developers of high-accuracy automated manufacturing systems for the fibre optics and wireless telecommunications industries, and does contract manufacturing for this sector. And it is one of the largest integrators of automated micro-manufacturing systems in the semiconductor and computer fields.

Another huge field is the electrical sector, developing systems for making motors, switches, transformers, and circuit breakers. The company also develops systems for packaging and manufacturing pharmaceuticals and consumer goods.

In 1997, Mr. Woerner won Canada's Entrepreneur of the Year Award from Ernst & Young.

Opportunities and Challenges

As manufacturers continue to look for ways to cut costs and improve efficiency, more and more will look to automation as well as outsourcing as a solution. ATS Automation Tooling is there on both fronts, which gives it solid long-term potential.

Its market is global, with 70 percent of sales south of the border, 8 percent in Canada, 13 percent in Europe, and 9 percent in the Pacific Rim. Thirty-nine percent of revenues come from the automotive sector, 45 percent from computers and electronics, 11 percent from health care, and 5 percent from other areas.

The company is dedicated to after-service and support, and 75 percent of its customers are repeat buyers. Twenty-three percent of revenues in 2000 came from just three customers, but this concentration is down from 30 percent in 1999. The company's major challenge is to continue expanding its reach into its newest markets, the fields of fibre optics, semiconductors, and health care.

As of March 31, 2001, ATS had $212 million in backlogged orders, representing almost a third of its annual sales volume.

Financial Highlights

Despite consistent growth in earnings and revenues, ATS's price has fluctuated broadly, dropping from a high of $40 in September 2000 to a low of $20 in December 2000. However, it was not as badly affected as other science and technology stocks, many of which dropped 70 to 90 percent. The stock traded in a flat range between $22 and $28 for the first half of 2001 despite continuing solid growth of revenues and earnings. As the economy improves, so should ATS's share price.

ATS Automation Tooling Systems Inc. at a Glance

Fiscal Year-end: March

7-Year Return: 35.7%

	1997	1998	1999	2000	2001	8-Year Growth Average (%)	8-Year Growth Total (%)
Revenue ($ mlns.)	249.8	402.9	515.3	530.0	679.0	33.9	627.0
Net Income ($ mlns.)	19.6	27.4	40.2	37.1	46.2	40.4	842.9
Earnings/ Share ($)	0.38	0.50	0.70	0.64	0.76	25.7	347.1
Dividend/ Share ($)	–	–	–	–	–	–	–
Price/ Earnings	17.1 - 32.9	20.4 - 60.3	13.6 - 37.1	16.4 - 51.6	24.9 - 53.3	–	–

Table data courtesy of ✓*Canadian Shareowner* **www.shareowner.com**

Stock Growth (Fiscal Year High-Low-Close)

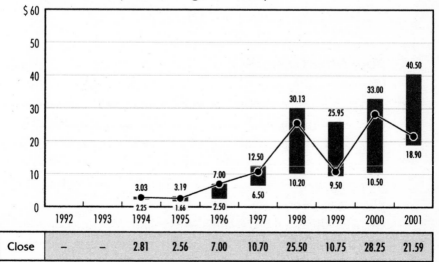

Close	–	–	2.81	2.56	7.00	10.70	25.50	10.75	28.25	21.59

MAGNA INTERNATIONAL INC.

337 Magna Drive
Aurora, ON L4G 7K1

Tel: (905) 726-2462	Employees: 62,000
Fax: (905) 726-7164	Founded: 1957
www.magna.ca	Listed: 1962
Symbol: MG.A (TSE) (Also MGA - NYSE)	

Chairperson: Frank Stronach
Vice-Chairperson and CEO: Belinda Stronach
President and COO: James Nicol

Share Price Growth	★ ★ ★ ★ ★
Revenue Growth	★ ★ ★ ★
EPS Growth	★ ★ ★ ★ ★
MG.A	**14**

About the Company

Three years after immigrating from Austria in 1954, Frank Stronach started a one-man tool and die shop, Multimatic. By the end of the year he had 10 employees and $13,000 in sales. From that humble beginning evolved a global industrial empire with 62,000 employees working in 166 factories and 31 research and development centres in 18 countries. Magna is one of the largest diversified auto parts suppliers in the world, and designs, engineers, and manufactures just about anything and everything that goes into making a car.

The company got sidetracked with non-core investments as it grew, but restructured in 1990–91, selling off most of its non-strategic divisions. It went on to expand its core business through the acquisition of a number of European auto systems suppliers, including Steyr-Daimler-Puch, now Magna Steyr. The company's growth strategy has been to add to the number of different auto parts it makes. So, even during the auto industry's periodic slumps, Magna has enhanced or maintained sales by increasing component contributions to various makes of car. Revenues have grown from just over $1.5 billion in 1990 to over $15.7 billion in 2000.

Operating divisions include Decoma—plastic modules and systems; Cosma—metal parts and assemblies; Magna Mirrors; Intier Automotive—interiors including seats, instrument panels, and insulation; Magna Steyr—drivetrain components and vehicle engineering and assembly; and Tesma—engine, powertrain, fuelling, and cooling components.

Magna International is Canada's third-largest spender on research and development in dollar terms—$246.5 million in 2000. However, because of its huge sales, R&D as a percentage of sales is actually quite low—1.6 percent. Among Magna's interesting R&D developments is hydroforming technology, a manufacturing process that uses water pressure to bend and form metal, and the built-in child safety seat, co-developed by Magna, which was named one of the great innovations of the 1980s by the Smithsonian Institute.

Mr. Stronach was honoured with the Order of Canada in 1999 and received the Ontario Lifetime Achievement Award from the Ernst & Young Entrepreneur of the Year program in 2000.

Opportunities and Challenges

In 2000, 73 percent of Magna's sales were to the big three U.S. automakers. The European market provides 11 percent of current revenue and Asia 3 percent, offering the best opportunity for future growth, and Magna has, in fact, been actively expanding its European presence. An improved economy in 2002 should continue to add to the company's value.

Magna has successfully created shareholder value in the past by spinning off its Tesma and Decoma divisions as new public companies. This "spinco" strategy, as Magna calls it, is meant to foster creativity and excellence among employees and management through equity and profit-sharing incentives tied directly to the division's focus of operations. It also decentralizes operations and avoids the build-up of bureaucracy. Magna continued this strategy by spinning off Intier on August 9, 2001, and plans the same for Magna Steyr in the future.

One of the big challenges facing Magna is management succession. Mr. Stronach's son Andrew was more interested in the horse-racing industry and took over Magna Entertainment, but daughter Belinda has been groomed for years to eventually take over Magna International from her father. She was appointed CEO in February 2001. Big shoes to fill, but Ms. Stronach looks to have the moxie to do the job.

Financial Highlights

Magna's stock hit a peak over $110 in the first half of 1998 and then steadily declined to the $60 level, despite growing revenues and earnings. In 2001 investors recognized Magna's undervalued state, and the shares have risen steadily to push $100 by mid-2001, in spite of a softening auto market and flat sales and earnings growth.

Magna International Inc. at a Glance

Fiscal Year-end: December

10-Year Return: 27.6%

	1996	1997	1998	1999	2000	10-Year Growth Average (%)	10-Year Growth Total (%)
Revenue ($ mlns.)	5,856.2	7,691.8	9,190.8	13,514.8	15,764.0	26.1	681.5
Net Income ($ mlns.)	309.0	427.4	461.1	620.9	744.4	81.8	4,411.5
Earnings/ Share ($)	4.71	5.39	5.51	6.86	7.97	45.9	1,274.1
Dividend/ Share ($)	1.08	1.14	1.28	1.32	1.86	34.9	830.0
Price/ Earnings	11.1 - 14.9	11.4 - 17.4	15 - 20.5	8.6 - 14	6.9 - 10	–	–

Table data courtesy of Canadian Shareowner   www.shareowner.com

Stock Growth (Fiscal Year High-Low-Close)

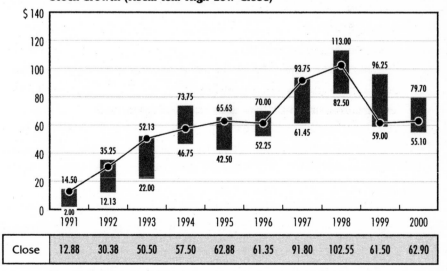

Close	12.88	30.38	50.50	57.50	62.88	61.35	91.80	102.55	61.50	62.90

Note: Beginning in fiscal 1999, the company's fiscal year-end changed from July to December. The months from August to December 1998 are not included in these data. Dividend growth figures are based on nine years.

BOMBARDIER INC.

800 René-Lévesque Blvd. West, 29th Floor
Montreal, QC H3B 1Y8

Tel: (514) 861-9481   Employees: 79,000
Fax: (514) 861-7053   Founded: 1942
www.bombardier.com   Listed: 1946
Symbol: BBD.B (TSE)

Chairperson: Laurent Beaudoin
President and CEO: Robert L. Brown

Share Price Growth	★ ★ ★ ★ ★
Revenue Growth	★ ★ ★
EPS Growth	★ ★ ★ ★
BBD.B	**12**

About the Company

When J.-Armande Bombardier invented the snowmobile, producing the seven-passenger prototype B-7 in 1937, he had no idea that
it was the genesis of a multi-billion dollar business. Commercialization
of this invention with the formation of his company in 1942 proved
a boon to the forestry, mining, and petroleum industries, which often
operate in remote and difficult terrain. But the company really made
strides with the invention of the personal snowmobile—the Ski-
Doo—which debuted in 1959 and created a whole new winter sport.
Mr. Bombardier was fortunate enough to see the growing success of
his work before he passed away in 1964.

The company expanded rapidly in the 1970s with the acquisition of Austrian Lohnerwerke Gmbh and exportation of the Ski-Doo to the U.S. In 1974 Bombardier diversified into mass transit with a contract to build rolling stock for Montreal's metro. This was followed by the acquisition of several railcar design and manufacturing operations in the U.S. and Europe in the 1980s.

The 1980s also saw the company move into the aerospace business with the takeover of Canadair as well as the acquisition of Short Brothers PLC, the Irish aircraft manufacturer that had secured the first aircraft production contract in history from the Wright Brothers. In the 1990s Bombardier bought out Learjet and de Havilland.

Today the company has five operating divisions: Bombardier Aerospace, Bombardier Transportation, Bombardier Recreational Products, Bombardier Capital, and Bombardier International, with plants in 12 countries. The company also owns and operates the J.-Armande Bombardier Museum in Valcourt, Que., the largest privately owned science and technology museum in Canada.

Bombardier had the 10th-largest R&D expenditure in Canada in 2000 at $132.2 million, which was only 1.0 percent of its sales.

Opportunities and Challenges

The company's operations are concentrated in Europe and North America, and it hasn't even begun to tap the huge Asian market. The function of its International division is just that—to expand the company with specific interest in Asia, Eastern and Central Europe, Russia, and Latin America. Bombardier maintains an office in Beijing as well as in Montreal.

With its keen eye for strategic acquisitions, the company should be able to follow through on its expansion plans. The company had an order backlog of $31.7 billion at the end of fiscal 2001.

The company is facing stiff competition in the regional jet aircraft market from Embraer SA of Brazil. The Brazilian government has supported Embraer's efforts through a program called Pro-Ex that provides low-interest loans to purchasers. Although Canada has successfully challenged Brazilian actions to the World Trade Organization in the past, Brazil modified its program sufficiently to win a ruling in June 2001 declaring that Pro-Ex was within trade rules.

Bombardier, with its strong political connection to the Liberals in Ottawa, has managed to secure similar cut-rate financing despite reservations from some cabinet ministers. The company faces a serious risk in accepting government favours. Canadian taxpayers will not be happy to see such a powerful and wealthy company (third-largest by market cap in Canada) bailed out while individuals are still skewered by high taxes. Somewhere the gravy train must end, and that could adversely affect Bombardier.

Financial Highlights

Except for a modest 20 percent retreat between July 2000 and April 2001, Bombardier stock has been on a steady upwards trend since 1993. This is a solid company for long-term investment.

Bombardier Inc. at a Glance

Fiscal Year-end: January
10-Year Return: 33.6%

	1997	1998	1999	2000	2001	10-Year Growth Average (%)	10-Year Growth Total (%)
Revenue ($ mlns.)	7,975.7	8,508.9	11,500.1	13,618.5	16,100.6	20.8	426.4
Net Income ($ mlns.)	403.9	407.8	517.1	711.3	944.6	28.2	801.3
Earnings/ Share ($)	0.29	0.29	0.38	0.52	0.69	26.0	666.7
Dividend/ Share ($)	0.05	0.08	0.09	0.11	0.14	25.6	600.0
Price/ Earnings	15.1 - 22.8	21.4 - 29.3	18.5 - 31.3	18.2 - 31	20.1 - 38.7	–	–

Table data courtesy of Canadian Shareowner   www.shareowner.com

Stock Growth (Fiscal Year High-Low-Close)

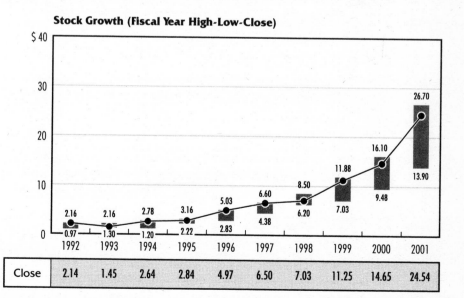

GENNUM CORPORATION

P.O. Box 489, Station A
Burlington, ON L7L 3Y3

Tel: (905) 632-2996
Fax: (905) 632-2055
www.gennum.com
Symbol: GND (TSE)

Employees: 491
Founded: 1973
Listed: 1982

President and CEO: Ian L. McWalter

Share Price Growth		★ ★ ★ ★ ★
Revenue Growth		★ ★ ★
EPS Growth		★ ★ ★ ★
GND		12

About the Company

Gennum is a high technology company focused on two separate areas: technology for the hearing impaired, and video processing and distribution for the television broadcasting industry. More specifically, the company designs and manufactures electronic components—silicon integrated circuits and thick-film hybrid circuits—for these systems.

Video components made up about 52 percent of its sales in fiscal 2000, with hearing instruments making up 47 percent and datacom products making up the remaining 1 percent.

The company was founded in 1973 and since then has grown revenues at an average of over 20 percent a year through 2000, though growth was slower in the last two years. It spends over 20 percent of sales on research and development.

Gennum has two production facilities in Burlington, Ont., and opened a new design centre in Ottawa in the first quarter of 2001. The company has also purchased a 12-acre parcel in Burlington for a new 68,000-square-foot facility to be completed by the first quarter of 2002. This will house 300 employees and accommodate the company's expansion for the next three to five years.

Opportunities and Challenges

As baby boomers start to lose their hearing after years of abusing their ears with loud rock concerts, boom boxes, and blaring Walkmans, Gennum is there to fill the need for hearing equipment. The company released Paragon Digital, its first line of digital signal processing components for hearing instruments, in April 2001. The patent-pending technology delivers superior-quality sound with low power consumption. These components are among the smallest on the market, allowing for complete "in-the-canal" hearing aids. Digital hearing aids are the fastest growing segment of the hearing instrument market.

Also in April, the company signed a two-year agreement with Tyco Electronics of Harrisburg, Penn. Tyco is one of the world's largest electronic components manufacturers, and the agreement will see joint marketing of Tyco's high-speed interconnect products and Gennum's multi-gigabit data communications technology. These both facilitate high-speed networking solutions for data transmission. The datacom market is only a minor part of Gennum's current product mix, but with the Tyco deal, could grow significantly from its current 1 percent.

The company faced a slowdown in sales for the first quarter of 2001 as demand tailed off for analog hearing aids. Sales of video equipment also slowed as customers reduced excess inventory of high-definition video equipment.

Although the company spends a lot of money on research, it failed to move quickly with the switch to digital hearing equipment. The biggest challenge for Gennum will be to keep on top of changes in the marketplace and to regain a leadership position. The release of the Paragon product is a step in this direction.

Financial Highlights

Gennum's stock moved in a broad trading range between $14 and $20 throughout 1999 and most of 2000 before slumping to a $12.50 to $13.50 trading range in October 2000. It started to move up again in January 2001 and has been on a steady, albeit somewhat erratic, uptrend since then, despite revenues and earnings falling off with the decline in the economy.

Gennum Corporation at a Glance

Fiscal Year-end: November

8-Year Return: 34.1%

	1996	1997	1998	1999	2000	8-Year Growth Average (%)	8-Year Growth Total (%)
Revenue ($ mlns.)	53.5	61.5	83.5	93.6	106.5	21.6	287.3
Net Income ($ mlns.)	9.7	11.9	16.2	17.5	18.8	24.3	337.2
Earnings/ Share ($)	0.27	0.33	0.45	0.49	0.53	24.3	341.7
Dividend/ Share ($)	0.05	0.06	0.08	0.09	0.12	22.5	100.0
Price/ Earnings	11.1 - 33.3	23.9 - 35.8	18.7 - 32.6	27.3 - 42.2	22.2 - 36.8	–	–

Table data courtesy of ✓*Canadian Shareowner* **www.shareowner.com**

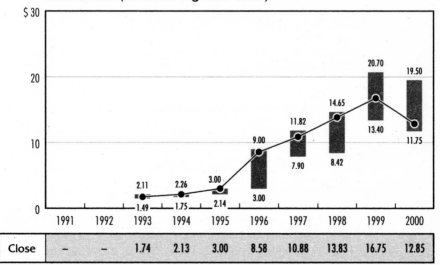

Stock Growth (Fiscal Year High-Low-Close)

Close	–	–	1.74	2.13	3.00	8.58	10.88	13.83	16.75	12.85
	1991	1992	1993	1994	1995	1996	1997	1998	1999	2000

SILENT WITNESS ENTERPRISES LTD.

6554-176th Street
Surrey, BC V3S 4G5

Tel: (604) 574-1526   Employees: 125
Fax: (604) 574-7736   Founded: 1985
www.silentwitness.com   Listed: 1987
Symbol: SWE (TSE) (Also SILW-NASDAQ)

Chairperson, President, and CEO: Rajeev (Rob) Bakshi

Share Price Growth	★ ★ ★ ★
Revenue Growth	★ ★ ★ ★
EPS Growth	★ ★ ★
SWE	**11**

About the Company

You've probably seen this scenario in the movies: robbers enter a bank, notice the security camera, and blow it away. But not if the bank were using one of the high tech, super-durable V-100 Bullet Resistant cameras from Silent Witness. This baby can withstand an attack from a 9 mm handgun or even a shotgun blast! The V-100 is just one of many award-winning, closed-circuit television security systems made by Silent Witness.

Founded in 1986 as a manufacturer of video-monitoring systems for buses (in which it remains the world leader with over 100,000 installed systems), the company expanded its product line over the years to provide security solutions for commercial businesses, security firms, casinos, prisons, schools, universities, warehouses, loading docks, emergency vehicles, transit, and taxicabs.

Products include The Puck (because it vaguely looks like one), an infrared illumination unit that enables pictures in complete darkness at up to 40 feet. The company also makes mini-cams, including a pinhole camera for covert operations.

Silent Witness underwent tremendous growth from 1995 through 2000, with a compound average sales growth of 57 percent and earnings growth of 158 percent. It was featured as one of the fastest-growing companies in Canada in the Profit 100 list released in the spring of 2001. Over 80 percent of sales are to the U.S., and the company was one of several honoured at the Canada Export Awards in October 2000.

Opportunities and Challenges

In 2000, the company positioned itself for a new wave of growth by embracing both digital and wireless technologies. Seven percent of revenues goes into research, and the company foresees tremendous opportunities in real-time video surveillance over the Internet, among other things.

Digital technology is replacing analog at an accelerating pace in the video field, and Silent Witness introduced its revolutionary SWC40R intelligent camera system in fiscal 2000. This digital unit compares successive frames of video to detect motion and only records frames when motion is detected.

In April 2001, the company acquired Gyyr's Pan/Tilt/Zoom (PTZ) product line along with associated intellectual property. The PTZ market is expected to hit $134 million by 2004.

The company opened an OEM (original equipment manufacturing) division in 2000 to leverage its video expertise beyond the securities business. It partnered with Stanley Works in November 2000 to develop and manufacture a digital video sensor for automatic doors under the Stanley trademark.

Quarterly revenues to April 30, 2001 showed that the company's sales outside North America increased 32 percent, revealing a large and largely untapped market.

The video surveillance market is large, with over $3 billion in annual sales. Silent Witness, for all its high-end expertise, only has a small portion of this total, because major players such as Sony, Panasonic, and JVC have most of the low-end market. The major challenge for Silent Witness is to continue to expand and grow its niche. The company moved to enter the budget market in June 2001with the release of the Sigma M12 surveillance unit, suited for small business, residential, and daycare applications.

Financial Highlights

Silent Witness fell precipitously from a high of $14.50 to a low of $7.00 during the technology downturn and has since climbed into a trading range between $9 and $11. Although share price was hit by the crash, revenues and earnings were not, and continued to grow into 2001, though the pace has slowed. Silent Witness has moved to enhance shareowner value by moving to buy back up to 4.9 percent of its shares between July 19, 2001 and July 19, 2002.

Silent Witness Enterprises at a Glance

Fiscal Year-end: July

4-Year Return: 60.4%

	1996	1997	1998	1999	2000	5-Year Growth Average (%)	5-Year Growth Total (%)
Revenue ($ mlns.)	8.3	13.4	21.7	34.0	40.2	49.6	384.3
Net Income ($ mlns.)	n/a	1.0	2.2	4.4	5.1	75.5	410.0
Earnings/ Share ($)	-0.25	0.18	0.37	0.65	0.75	–	–
Dividend/ Share ($)	–	–	–	–	–	–	–
Price/ Earnings	-4 - -8.3	4.4 - 10.8	5 - 17.2	6.5 - 22.8	9.7 - 19.3	–	–

Table data courtesy of ✓*Canadian Shareowner* **www.shareowner.com**

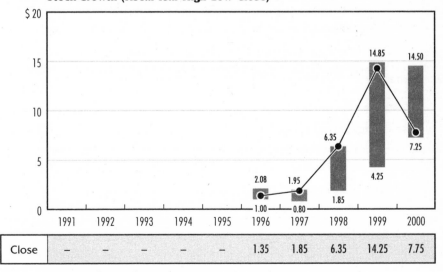

Stock Growth (Fiscal Year High-Low-Close)

Close	–	–	–	–	–	1.35	1.85	6.35	14.25	7.75
	1991	1992	1993	1994	1995	1996	1997	1998	1999	2000

Note: Data for 1996 from company reports.

BW TECHNOLOGIES LTD.

242-3030 3rd Avenue N.E.
Calgary, AB T2A 6T7

Tel: (403) 248-9226   Employees: 116
Fax: (403) 273-3708   Founded: 1987
www.gasmonitors.com   Listed: 1997
Symbol: BWT (TSE)

President and CEO: Cody Z. Slater

Share Price Growth		★ ★ ★
Revenue Growth		★ ★ ★
EPS Growth		★ ★
BWT		**8**

About the Company

Since it was founded in 1987, Calgary-based BW Technologies has grown into a world leader in gas-detection technologies. Its products are used primarily by the oil industry and other industrial customers to detect noxious gases that might endanger employees or create a hazardous situation. They include portable units the size of a cell-phone as well as fixed units and stand-alone wireless units.

BW is also involved in other markets, including heating, ventilation, and air conditioning, and underground parking garages. In August 2000, the company won a lucrative contract to design and manufacture custom systems for the Eurotunnel, the rail link between England and France.

The company has offices in Texas and the U.K. as well as in Calgary and a network of authorized dealers with over 400 offices in over 50 countries. In January 2001, BW Technologies was named as one of the 30 fastest-growing companies in Alberta by *Alberta Venture Magazine* for the third consecutive year. It's also listed in the Profit 100.

Opportunities and Challenges

In 2001, the company expanded beyond the industrial market into the commercial arena with a product that detects carbon monoxide and other gases in underground parking garages. Current systems require frequent and expensive manual calibration, but BW's detectors are maintenance-free and can be connected to the standard control systems manufactured by Honeywell, Siemens, and Johnson Controls. After three years, the detectors are replaced like a light bulb. This promises to be a lucrative and growing market with repeat business built-in.

The company also incorporated multimedia cards (used in MP3 players and digital cameras) into its GasAlert Max monitors so that data can be logged continuously. These units record data more frequently, can store more data, and are 30 percent cheaper than their competitors. By allowing the recording of real-time details, this technology allows BW to pursue the telecom and utilities market it was previously unable to serve.

Gas detection equipment is in high demand in the oil industry, and the ongoing boom in the oil patch should continue to drive a good portion of BW's revenues. However, a drop in oil prices, coupled with a fall-off in exploration, could impact BW's sales. Diversification into the home heating and air conditioning field as well as underground parking should mitigate this possibility.

Financial Highlights

BW Technologies was one of the few technology companies that gained in price during the NASDAQ bear market, and it hit new highs in the first quarter of 2001 at the technology market bottom. After a sharp correction in May and June 2001, a record first-quarter report sent BW's stock back on its upward trend again.

BW Technologies Ltd. at a Glance

Fiscal Year-end: April

2-Year Return: 37.7%

	1997	1998	1999	2000	2001	4-Year Growth Average (%)	4-Year Growth Total (%)
Revenue ($ mlns.)	–	12.3	17.3	18.4	27.8	32.5	125.1
Net Income ($ mlns.)	–	0.6	1.2	1.2	2.8	79.0	374.0
Earnings/ Share ($)	–	0.15	0.28	0.25	0.49	57.3	226.7
Dividend/ Share ($)	–	–	–	–	–	–	–
Price/ Earnings	–	12.3 - 30	8.9 - 17.3	18 - 34	9.4 - 21.2	–	–

Table data courtesy of Canadian Shareowner www.shareowner.com

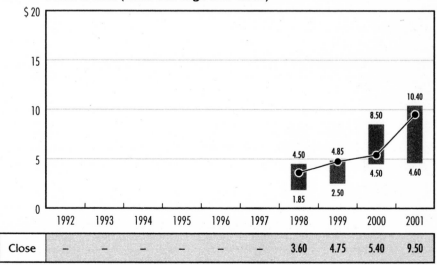

Note: Data for the years 1998 and 2001 from company reports.

DUPONT CANADA INC.

P.O. Box 2200, Streetsville
Mississauga, ON L5M 2H3

Tel: (905) 821-5679
Fax: (905) 821-5653
www.dupont.ca
Symbol: DUP.A (TSE)

Employees: 3,300
Founded: 1862
Listed: 1961

Chairperson, President, and CEO: David W. Colcleugh
Vice-President and CFO: Bill Matthews

Share Price Growth	★ ★ ★ ★
Revenue Growth	★
EPS Growth	★ ★ ★
DUP.A	8

About the Company

If the term "venerable" can be applied to a science and technology company, it describes DuPont. Some of its innovative chemical and petroleum products have even become part of the English language. Who hasn't heard of nylon, Lycra, or Teflon? The American giant is one of the world's great businesses.

But what of DuPont Canada? The company traces its history back to the Hamilton Powder Company, founded in 1862. In 1867, Lammot du Pont bought shares in the company and became a director. This injection of capital and expertise enabled the company to become a leading supplier of the explosives needed to build Canada's emerging railways.

The company amalgamated with several others as Canadian Explosives Limited in 1910 and supplied a large portion of the munitions for Canada's war effort in World War I. After the war it acquired three Canadian subsidiaries of E.I. du Pont de Nemours and became Canadian Industries Limited (CIL). In 1954, a U.S. antitrust settlement split the company into two: CIL and DuPont Canada. DuPont Canada debuted on the Toronto Stock Exchange in December 1961.

Today, the company manufactures products for the Canadian market and for export in six manufacturing plants. It operates five divisions: Nylon Enterprise, Performance Coatings and Polymers, Specialty Fibres, Specialty Materials, and Specialty Polymers and Films. These units make products as diverse as nylon yarn (such brands as Antron and Stainmaster), paints for the automotive industry, Kevlar (used in bulletproof vests), herbicides, and plastic films such as Mylar.

The Canadian subsidiary is more than just a branch plant that produces the stuff invented at DuPont's U.S. operations. It runs one of the few materials science R&D centres in Canada at its Kingston plant, employing 190 people. Among the inventions and developments coming out of DuPont Canada are specialty air bag yarns, aseptic pouch packaging, and the nylon heat exchanger. DuPont's Kingston plant, in fact, is the largest manufacturer of air bag yarns in the world.

Opportunities and Challenges

The nylon heat exchanger invented at DuPont's Kingston plant has a number of interesting commercial possibilities, including nylon radiators for cars. Such a radiator could be moulded to fit where convenient in a car rather than sitting as a bulky up-front unit. This would offer space and design improvements for auto manufacturers. Commercial production of heat exchanger products is slated to start sometime in 2001.

One of the more interesting developments at DuPont is the creation of a new Fuel Cells unit to supply materials and components to this emerging market. Proton exchange membrane fuel cells are expected to be a $10-billion-a-year business by 2010. DuPont has been providing advanced materials for the fuel cells used in space travel for over 35 years, so it is no stranger to the business. The company is also active in the development of direct methanol fuel cell technology.

DuPont Canada is a dynamic and innovative company with deep pockets and a track record going back over 100 years. It is not likely to be a go-go big mover like some up-and-coming technology companies. What it does offer the investor is a solid and dependable investment that is likely to generate good returns for many years to come.

Financial Highlights

DuPont managed to weather the tech downturn and was hitting new highs in the first quarter of 2001. While there have been some wide fluctuations, the general trend for the stock has been upwards since 1982. An excellent long-term stock to buy and hang on to.

DuPont Canada Inc. at a Glance

Fiscal Year-end: December
10-Year Return: 20.8%

	1996	1997	1998	1999	2000	10-Year Growth Average (%)	10-Year Growth Total (%)
Revenue ($ mlns.)	1,827.4	1,997.8	2,025.1	2,211.4	2,288.9	6.2	71.4
Net Income ($ mlns.)	200.0	212.1	219.9	252.7	269.5	20.1	381.3
Earnings/ Share ($)	0.72	0.76	0.79	0.91	0.97	20.2	385.0
Dividend/ Share ($)	0.17	1.18	0.21	0.23	0.28	70.0	250.0
Price/ Earnings	11 - 16.2	12.7 - 15.8	13.3 - 20	14.7 - 22	12 - 21.3	–	–

Table data courtesy of Canadian Shareowner   www.shareowner.com

Stock Growth (Fiscal Year High-Low-Close)

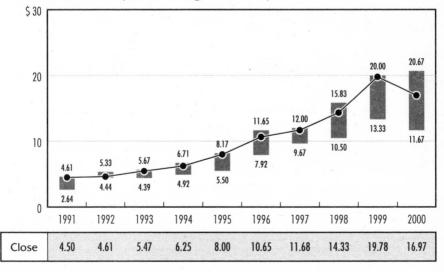

Close	4.50	4.61	5.47	6.25	8.00	10.65	11.68	14.33	19.78	16.97

CAE INC.

Royal Bank Plaza
Suite 3060, P.O. Box 30
Toronto, ON M5J 2J1

Tel: (416) 865-0070   Employees: 9,960
Fax: (416) 865-0337   Founded: 1947
www.cae.com   Listed: 1961
Symbol: CAE (TSE)

Chairperson: Lynton R. Wilson
President and CEO: Derek H. Burney

Share Price Growth	★
Revenue Growth	0
EPS Growth	★ ★ ★ ★ ★
CAE	6

About the Company

CAE Inc. is the world's major manufacturer of state-of-the-art flight simulators for pilot training. Its simulators not only reproduce the controls used on various aircraft, but also create as realistic a setting as possible in a complete immersion environment with a wraparound motion picture screen. The MAXVUE visual system uses computer-generated graphics that pilots see as an "out of the window" experience.

Simulators are built to duplicate a variety of aircraft, including Boeing, Airbus, and military helicopters. In 1997, the company won a 20-year contract to design, build, manage, and operate a training facility for Royal Air Force helicopter crews. This marked the first time that a complete military training function had been handed to a commercial contractor. The chopper training environment features six networked simulators and CAE's proprietary tactical simulation software. It can be used for tactical training and mission rehearsals with up to 500 computer-generated friendly and hostile craft on screen. The ultimate video game—but you have to join the Royal Air Force to play!

In April 2001 CAE opened a six-simulator training facility in São Paulo, the first independently owned and operated flight training centre in South America. Latin American airlines used to have to train pilots abroad, but can now train them close to home.

The company also manufactures marine control systems and is building the controls and instrumentation for the British Royal Navy's new Astute Class nuclear submarines. CAE was actually sub-contracted for the job by BAE Systems, another Canadian technology firm (formerly Canadian Marconi).

Another business unit for CAE is Forestry Systems, providing proprietary software, sensors, and control systems for optimizing sawmill operations, as well as screening solutions for the pulp and paper industry.

CAE has the 11th largest R&D budget in Canada, according to Re$earch Infosource.

Opportunities and Challenges

In October 1999, president and CEO Derek Burney joined the company with a mandate to enhance shareholder value. This he did in spades as he streamlined the business, discarding non-core operations and focusing on three distinct high-margin areas: commercial flight simulation and training, military simulation and controls, and forestry systems.

CAE was picked by Patrick McKeough of *The Successful Investor* as his "one stock" for the year 2000 in the *Globe and Mail*'s annual stock-picking contest, and it won, doubling in the year.

But its growth is hardly over. CAE only entered the lucrative pilot training business with the opening of its new Brazilian training centre. Pilot training is a $12 billion a year industry, 10 times CAE's current revenues, and as the leading manufacturer of flight simulators, CAE is well positioned to take much of this business. Some domestic training is currently conducted at the company's St. Laurent, Que., plant, but plans call for new training centres to be built in Toronto and in Spain. CAE also offers the only aviation training system available over the Internet.

As in any business that serves a particular commercial market, however, CAE's fortunes could go up or down in lockstep with the fortunes of the airline industry.

There is some concern that CAE stock is outpacing the company's growth. The P/E as of mid-2001 was a new high of 30.5, but this is, in my opinion, a fair multiple for a company showing solid and continuing growth, even in a weak economy.

CAE did not meet our minimum requirements in the revenue category. Revenues dropped sharply from $1,027.3 million in 1994 to $657.6 million in 1995, due to restructuring. Revenues and earnings have grown steadily since then, however, so we are making an allowance in this case.

Financial Highlights

A chart of CAE shows steady, almost straight-line growth since November 1999, while information technology, telecommunications, and Internet stocks were experiencing wild fluctuations. The company continues apace. The stock split two-for-one in June 2001.

CAE Inc. at a Glance

Fiscal Year-end: March

10-Year Return: 17.2%

	1997	1998	1999	2000	2001	10-Year Growth Average (%)	Total (%)
Revenue ($ mlns.)	867.3	922.4	1,070.1	1,164.3	1,191.4	2.9	13.9
Net Income ($ mlns.)	60.3	70.6	77.3	90.7	134.7	17.9	310.7
Earnings/ Share ($)	0.55	0.64	0.70	0.83	1.25	17.8	303.2
Dividend/ Share ($)	0.16	0.16	0.16	0.19	0.20	2.7	25.0
Price/ Earnings	17.5 - 22.9	15.9 - 20.4	11.1 - 19.5	8.8 - 20.5	10.2 - 20.8	–	–

Table data courtesy of ✓Canadian Shareowner   www.shareowner.com

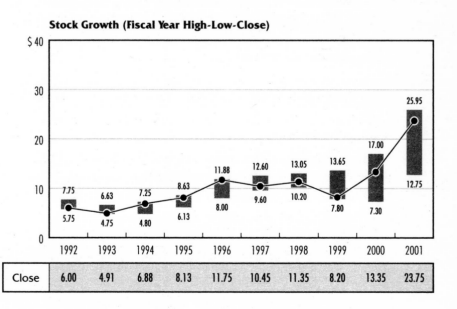

Stock Growth (Fiscal Year High-Low-Close)

	1992	1993	1994	1995	1996	1997	1998	1999	2000	2001
Close	6.00	4.91	6.88	8.13	11.75	10.45	11.35	8.20	13.35	23.75

TESMA INTERNATIONAL INC.

P.O. Box 895
Maple, ON L6A 1S8

Tel: (905) 669-7355   Employees: 4,418
Fax: (905) 738-1248   Founded: 1983
www.tesma.com   Listed: 1995
Symbol: TSM.A (TSE) (Also TSMA-NASDAQ)

President and CEO: Manfred Gingl

Share Price Growth	★ ★
Revenue Growth	★ ★ ★
EPS Growth	★
TSM.A	**6**

About the Company

Tesma originated in 1983 when auto parts giant Magna International combined five of its divisions involved in engines and transmissions into one unit, the Maple Group, renamed the Tesma International Group in 1988. In 1993, Tesma acquired its first manufacturing facility in Europe, and in 1995, Magna spun off this wholly owned subsidiary in an initial public offering.

Tesma continued to expand, taking over the Blau companies and their operations in Germany, Austria, Spain, and Canada in 1995, and Germany-based Eralmetall with its aluminum die-casting capabilities in 1997. Further acquisitions in Detroit strengthened its North

American operations, and the takeover of HAC Corporation of South Korea in 1999 gave it a toehold in Asia.

Tesma is focused on three areas—engines, transmissions, and fuel systems. It operates 22 manufacturing facilities and two research centres, shipping in excess of a billion dollars of product annually to OEMs on six continents.

Opportunities and Challenges

Outsourcing is gaining popularity in many industries, from electronics to pharmaceuticals to the automotive field. Tesma is well positioned to meet this growing demand in the global automotive market; its client list includes DaimlerChrysler, VW, Nissan, Audi, BMW, Daewoo, Fiat, Honda, and SAAB.

In May 2001, Tesma announced it was exploring a merger with Magna Steyr Group, which would increase its presence in the powertrain field.

Tesma's fortunes are tied to those of the automotive industry, although a diversified clientele makes it immune from troubles plaguing any one particular manufacturer. In fact, while the six months to January 31, 2001, saw a 10 percent decline in North American vehicle production, Tesma's sales increased by 7 percent because of new product lines which increased Tesma's content contribution to North American and European cars by 20 percent and 17 percent respectively. Export sales and aftermarket parts sales also contributed to the revenue growth.

A possible challenge in the future could be a large-scale shift to fuel-cell driven cars. Major auto manufacturers such as Ford and DaimlerChrysler are pouring lots of money into alternative fuel research and development. But Tesma should be more than up to such challenges as they materialize. Its R&D team is well experienced at developing fuel-efficient engines and low emissions fuel systems.

Financial Highlights

After the stock traded in a wide range between $15 and $23 from 1997 through the first quarter of 2000, investors finally clued in to the company's steadily growing revenues, and earnings and the stock advanced steadily from April to October of that year. A sharp correction late in the year was followed by a strong advance to new highs in the first half of 2001.

Tesma International Inc. at a Glance

Fiscal Year-end: July

5-Year Return: 30.3%

	1996	1997	1998	1999	2000	7-Year Growth Average (%)	7-Year Growth Total (%)
Revenue ($ mlns.)	455.6	551.5	645.9	893.7	1,127.8	26.3	302.4
Net Income ($ mlns.)	18.9	24.6	38.4	52.3	84.9	31.3	335.4
Earnings/ Share ($)	0.91	1.13	1.28	1.76	2.83	16.6	106.6
Dividend/ Share ($)	0.15	0.20	0.22	0.31	0.54	39.6	260.0
Price/ Earnings	7.1 - 11.5	8 - 20.1	13.3 - 18.8	8.2 - 12.8	5.8 - 11	–	–

Table data courtesy of  √Canadian Shareowner   www.shareowner.com

Stock Growth (Fiscal Year High-Low-Close)

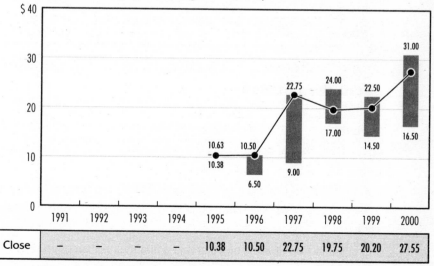

Close	–	–	–	–	10.38	10.50	22.75	19.75	20.20	27.55

Note: Dividend growth figures based on five years.

MAGELLAN AEROSPACE CORPORATION

3160 Derry Road East
Mississauga, ON L4T 1A9

Tel: (905) 677-1889
Fax: (905) 677-5658
www.malaero.com
Symbol: MAL (TSE)

Employees: 3,200
Founded: 1930
Listed: 1996

Chairperson and CEO: N. Murray Edwards
President and COO: Richard A. Neill

Share Price Growth	0
Revenue Growth	★ ★ ★
EPS Growth	★
MAL	4

About the Company

Founded in 1930 as Fleet Aerospace, the company underwent restructuring in 1995 as the commercial aviation industry started to recover from its longest slump ever. Retirement of debt, new equity financing, and new contracts from Southwest, Boeing, Bombardier, and McDonnell Douglas breathed new life into the veteran company. This was followed by a name change as the company went public in 1996.

Magellan Aerospace is now a world-class designer and manufacturer of high tech aerospace components and systems for the commercial and military aviation industries. The company maintains strong relationships with such aircraft manufacturers as Boeing, Airbus, Lockheed Martin, Bell Helicopter, and Northrop Grumman, and engine manufacturers such as Pratt & Whitney and Rolls Royce.

Magellan grew throughout the latter half of the 1990s, partly through the acquisition of a number of smaller aerospace companies. It now has 10 divisions throughout Canada and the U.S., operating under the Magellan umbrella but carrying their own corporate names. These include Fleet Industries (the original company), which specializes in bonded and sheet metal components and makes aircraft structures and sub-assemblies; Bristol Aerospace, which makes rockets and weapons systems (NASA has launched more than 800 Bristol-built rockets); Orenda, which specializes in gas turbine engine technology; and Langley Aerospace, which manufactures precision machined parts, including cryogenic seals and thrust gimbals for the space shuttle.

Magellan's proprietary products include exhaust systems, weapons systems, advanced materials, and a wire strike protection system to reduce helicopter accidents. Besides manufacturing, the company does overhaul and repair work for the Canadian and American military.

Opportunities and Challenges

The aviation business is on a roll right now as more and more people put long-distance travel into their vacation and recreation plans. Business travel is also increasing. Worldwide growth in air travel is expected to continue at 5 to 6 percent annually for the next 20 years.

As a result, all aspects of manufacturing, support, and services related to air travel have prospered. Companies as varied as CAE (flight simulators and pilot training) and Magellan Aerospace have hit new highs in the first half of 2001 and look to continue to prosper into the future.

A potentially lucrative new field for Magellan is power turbines. Its Orenda Aerospace division commissioned its first 2.5 megawatt gas turbine in June 2001, marking the company's re-entry into this field.

Deregulation of the power industry and the continuing power shortage in America should fuel growth.

Sixty-five percent of Magellan's business is Canadian, and the company's biggest challenge will be to grow its presence in the much larger U.S. market. It is already a solid player in the U.S. space program through Bristol and Langley Aerospace, and it has a good client base among U.S. aircraft manufacturers.

Magellan Aerospace did not meet all of our selection criteria, since it experienced losses from 1991 to 1995. But those losing years are far behind it, with the company turning a profit every year since 1996. The stock climbed strongly to $11.20 in 1997 before zigzagging steadily lower to January 2000, when it entered a broad range between $5.00 and $7.00. In April 2001 the stock started moving up again. Given this history, investors should monitor performance carefully and be prepared to sell if circumstances warrant.

A third of the company's sales are to Boeing, and the health of Boeing affects Magellan. Boeing's announcement of possible cutbacks in mid-July 2001 caused a price correction. While Magellan's revenues were up only modestly for the first quarter of 2001, earnings were up sharply on cost-cutting measures taken, lower interest rates, and liquidation of debt.

Financial Highlights

After trading in a two-year range of $5 to $7, the stock took off sharply to hit new 52-week highs in the first quarter of 2001 while other technology issues were tanking. As noted, a sharp correction followed on news of planned cutbacks by Boeing.

Magellan Aerospace Corporation at a Glance

Fiscal Year-end: December

10-Year Return: 5.7%

	1996	1997	1998	1999	2000	10-Year Growth Average (%)	10-Year Growth Total (%)
Revenue ($ mlns.)*	136.7	256.3	426.9	561.8	625.4	31.8	422.5
Net Income ($ mlns.)	14.6	15.5	32.3	42.8	37.9	–	–
Earnings/ Share ($)	0.37	0.30	0.54	0.68	0.59	–	–
Dividend/ Share ($)	–	–	–	–	–	–	–
Price/ Earnings	4.2 - 16.8	10.3 - 37.3	9.7 - 20.2	8.8 - 15.1	8.1 - 12.7	–	–

Table data courtesy of ✓*Canadian Shareowner* **www.shareowner.com**

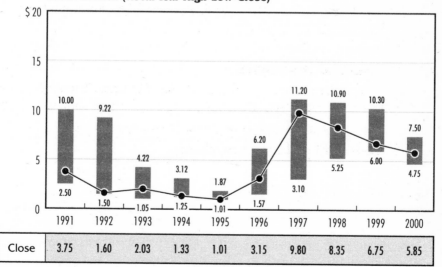

Stock Growth (Fiscal Year High-Low-Close)

Close	3.75	1.60	2.03	1.33	1.01	3.15	9.80	8.35	6.75	5.85

* Note: Revenue average growth excludes 1983, for which no data were available.

INFORMATION TECHNOLOGY

AOL Time Warner Inc.
CGI Group Inc.
Check Point Software Technologies Ltd.
EMC Corporation
Mercury Interactive Corporation
Microsoft Corporation
Network Appliance, Inc.
Siebel Systems, Inc.
Solectron Corporation
Yahoo! Inc.
Intel Corporation
Cognos Inc.
THQ Inc.
Sapient Corporation
ATI Technologies Inc.
Celestica Inc.
Internet Security Systems, Inc.
The Thomson Corporation

AOL Time Warner Inc.

75 Rockefeller Plaza
New York, NY 10019

Tel: (212) 484-4000
www.aoltimewarner.com
Symbol: AOL (NYSE)

Employees: 88,500
Founded: 1985 (AOL)
Listed: 1992

Chairperson: Steve Case
CEO: Gerald Levin

Share Price Growth	★ ★ ★ ★ ★
Revenue Growth	★ ★ ★ ★ ★
EPS Growth	★ ★ ★ ★ ★
AOL	**15**

About the Company

On January 11, 2001, one of the most significant corporate mergers in history took place when America Online merged with Time Warner to form AOL Time Warner. America Online is one of the pioneers in developing and promoting the Internet. With its ubiquitous free diskettes, and later free CDs, making it easy for just about anyone to get online, AOL grew by leaps and bounds, increasing revenues from US$21.4 million in 1991 to an incredible US$6,886.0 million in 2000. Earnings have risen steadily for the last three years.

With the merger complete, AOL Time Warner is a mega-media conglomerate with the following well-known brands in its stable: Home Box Office, Turner Broadcasting, CNN, Time, Warner Brothers, New

Line Cinema, Netscape, CompuServe, Atlantic Records, DC Comics, and of course, America Online. The company controls extensive cable television interests as well through Time Warner Cable and Turner Broadcasting.

I could write a mini-essay on each of these brands, but suffice to say that each is a powerhouse in its own right. And, joined at the hip as AOL Time Warner, they are even more formidable. With the convergence of the previously separate media of print, broadcasting, and Internet progressing at an accelerated clip, AOL Time Warner has three essential ingredients for success: Internet expertise, high-speed cable access to the end-user, and rich broadcasting and print content.

The company's mission is "to become the world's most respected and valued company by connecting, informing and entertaining people everywhere in innovative ways that will enrich their lives." A lofty goal, but one that it likely can achieve.

Opportunities and Challenges

With a market cap of over US$193 billion in mid-2001, AOL Time Warner ranks in the top 10 companies by market cap in the U.S., ahead of such giants as Cisco, Home Depot, IBM, and Coca-Cola. If the company can capitalize on the synergies between its various divisions, it can certainly achieve its goal of being top dog.

But with its large size, it will be tough to continue growing at the same pace as during the last 10 years. Microsoft is just under twice as large, and the largest U.S. company by market cap, General Motors, is just shy of two and half times as large. AOL's P/E ratio of around 80 in mid-2001 is larger than the P/Es of GE and Microsoft combined. So AOL's biggest challenge will be to grow earnings that justify its lofty price.

The data in our tables represent America Online before the merger. Although the company took a penny a share loss in 1997, revenue growth was strong from 1995 on. Time Warner, on the other hand, has had a very checkered fiscal record for a large organization, losing money every year from 1989 to 1998 before becoming profitable in 1999. The major question is whether the merger was a good deal for AOL. Will Time Warner prove to be an anchor on a ship destined to sail off to new glory?

Is AOL overpriced? The quarter to June 30, 2001 showed revenues up marginally, by 3 percent year-over-year on a pro-forma basis that assumes the merger had been completed a year earlier. Earnings before amortization of goodwill and one-time charges were up to US$0.32 from US$0.23 the year before. The company is feeling the pinch of declining ad sales in a weak economy. To bring its P/E down to Microsoft's level of 40, earnings must double. With earnings at US$0.39 a share for 2000—before the merger—much more is certainly possible. But a general turnaround in the economy will be required. The company has tremendous potential, but evaluate current circumstances before investing and have a plan for exiting if things turn ugly.

Financial Highlights

After trading to a high of US$95 in December 1999, AOL preceded most of the rest of the Internet sector in plunging down to US$50 by March 2000. The stock then traded up to US$74 briefly before settling into a broad trading range between US$35 and US$60. The stock is somewhat volatile, having navigated between those limits twice in the first half of 2001.

AOL Time Warner Inc. at a Glance

Fiscal Year-end: June

9-Year Return: 101.0%

	1996	1997	1998	1999	2000	10-Year Growth Average (%)	10-Year Growth Total (%)
Revenue (US$ mlns.)	1,093.9	1,685.2	2,600.0	4,777.0	6,886.0	103.0	32,077.6
Net Income (US$ mlns.)	51.9	-17.2	218.4	398.8	1,018.1	–	–
Earnings/ Share (US$)	0.03	-0.01	0.11	0.16	0.39	–	–
Dividend/ Share (US$)	–	–	–	–	–	–	–
Price/ Earnings	44.5 - 147.9	-139.8 - -388.3	32.1 - 124.7	53.9 - 548.4	98.6 - 245.7	–	–

Table data courtesy of ✓*Canadian Shareowner* www.shareowner.com

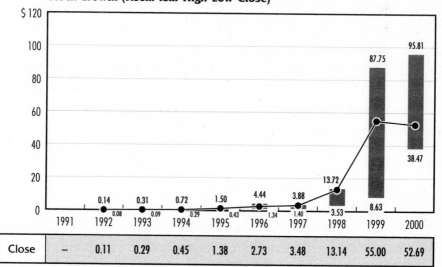

Stock Growth (Fiscal Year High-Low-Close)

	1991	1992	1993	1994	1995	1996	1997	1998	1999	2000
Close	–	0.11	0.29	0.45	1.38	2.73	3.48	13.14	55.00	52.69

Note: These data reflect AOL only, before its merger with Time Warner.

CGI GROUP INC.

1130 Sherbrooke Street West, 5th Floor
Montreal, QC H3A 2M8

Tel: (514) 841-3200   Employees: 10,000
Fax: (514) 841-3299   Founded: 1976
www.cgi.ca   Listed: 1986
Symbol: GIB.A (TSE) (Also GIB-NYSE)

Chairperson, President, and CEO: Serge Godin
Executive Vice-President, and CFO: André Imbeau

Share Price Growth	★ ★ ★ ★ ★
Revenue Growth	★ ★ ★ ★ ★
EPS Growth	★ ★ ★ ★ ★
GIB.A	**15**

About the Company

Founded in 1976 by Serge Godin and André Imbeau, CGI Group Inc.
started as a modest Quebec City consulting firm with six employees
and revenues of $138,000. From there it has grown to become the
fifth-largest IT services provider in North America and the largest in
Canada, with annual revenues of $1.4 billion in 2000. Acquisitions
have given it a global presence, with project offices across Canada as
well as in the U.S., the U.K., and 20 other countries.

The company offers complete end-to-end IT services and business
solutions with a focus on large-scale, multi-year renewable contracts.
Services include implementing computer infrastructure on-site or

through CGI's data centre, installation of custom-designed programming solutions, systems integration, and service and maintenance of on-site computer networks.

Contracts in the first half of 2001 included infrastructure outsourcing for American aluminum products manufacturer Pechiney Group, implementation of CGI's Global Insurance Open Solution for Economical Insurance, and a $300 million agreement with Laurentian Bank to take over the development and management of its information technology services. CGI's order backlog stands at $8.2 billion.

In 1994 CGI became the first IT services company in North America to get ISO 9001 certification for its project management framework. The company was recognized as Services Provider of the Year by Microsoft in 2000.

Opportunities and Challenges

Outsourcing continues to be a favourite cost-cutting measure for many companies, and CGI serves this growing market. The company continues to make strategic acquisitions: IMRglobal in early 2001 added high-end consultancy capabilities in the U.S. and U.K. as well as a presence in France, India, Japan, and Australia; and CyberBranch is a California company with expertise in Web-based solutions for credit unions.

CGI Group had a stellar year in 1999 as a result of Y2K remediation work. As a result, business dried up somewhat in 2000. Revenues showed little growth over 1999 and earnings per share declined 32 percent. The quarterly report to March 31, 2001, showed revenues off 1.7 percent from the year previous, partly due to additional Y2K work in the first quarter of 2000. First quarter earnings were off 44 percent, but were ahead of expectations and improved from the final quarter of 2000.

The slowdown in the technology arena has also affected CGI, but may work to its advantage as companies feeling the pinch look to IT outsourcing to cut costs. CGI is aggressively working to capitalize on these opportunities.

Financial Highlights

CGI stock crashed severely in the tech wreck, from a high of $34 to a low of $6. The first half of 2001 saw the stock yo-yo between the $5 and $10 levels, settling at the upper end of that range in mid-July. The company is still adjusting from its Y2K-induced boom and starting to solidify its momentum going forward again.

CGI Group Inc. at a Glance

Fiscal Year-end: September

5-Year Return: 80.0%

	1996	1997	1998	1999	2000	8-Year Growth Average (%)	8-Year Growth Total (%)
Revenue ($ mlns.)	122.0	231.9	741.0	1,409.5	1,436.0	64.8	1,784.5
Net Income ($ mlns.)	2.7	7.8	34.8	83.8	55.7	142.1	13,825.0
Earnings/ Share ($)	0.02	0.05	0.15	0.32	0.21	–	–
Dividend/ Share ($)	–	–	–	–	–	–	–
Price/ Earnings	9.2 - 23.4	8.1 - 97.5	28 - 115.3	25.4 - 59.5	41.9 - 164	–	–

Table data courtesy of *Canadian Shareowner*   www.shareowner.com

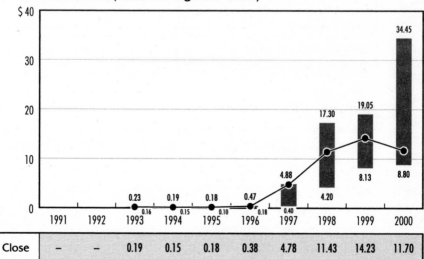

Stock Growth (Fiscal Year High-Low-Close)

| Close | – | – | 0.19 | 0.15 | 0.18 | 0.38 | 4.78 | 11.43 | 14.23 | 11.70 |

CHECK POINT SOFTWARE TECHNOLOGIES LTD.

Three Lagoon Drive, Suite 400
Redwood City, CA 94065

Tel: (650) 628-2000
Fax: (650) 654-4233
www.checkpoint.com
Symbol: CHKP (NASDAQ)

Employees: 1,100
Founded: 1993
Listed: 1996

Founder, Chairperson, and CEO: Gil Schwed
Founder and Senior Vice-President: Marius Nacht
President: Jerry Ungerman

Share Price Growth	★ ★ ★ ★ ★
Revenue Growth	★ ★ ★ ★ ★
EPS Growth	★ ★ ★ ★ ★
CHKP	**15**

About the Company

The biggest concern for businesses establishing an online presence or integrating local and wide area networks with the Internet is security. Sensitive data must be protected from the prying eyes of hackers. Transactions involving money transfer must be secure. And so business has turned in droves to Check Point Software Technologies for virtual private networks (VPNs), firewalls, and other leading-edge security solutions.

Check Point virtually invented Internet security. Founded by two Israelis, Gil Schwed and Marius Nacht, in 1993, today Check Point dominates the world of VPNs. A virtual private network connects local area networks together over a public network such as the Internet through encrypted connections. This is considerably cheaper than installing dedicated circuits for a true private network. Check Point's VPN solutions command 62 percent of market share, with runner-up Nortel a distant second at 15 percent.

Before founding Check Point, Mr. Schwed cut his technological teeth working for Israeli optical inspection firm Oprotech, National Semiconductor, and the Israeli Defense Forces. In 1994 the company released Check Point Firewall-1, now the standard in enterprise-wide network security. Check Point was first with VPN solutions and leads the market in VPN installations. Schwed also holds the patent for Stateful Inspection, another Internet security application.

In 1997, Check Point launched the Open Platform for Security (OPSEC)—an open architecture that provides the framework for the integration and interoperability of solutions from over 270 in-dustry partners. Products developed by members of the OPSEC Alliance go through rigorous testing before being approved as "OPSEC Certified" or "Secured by Check Point." These solutions are value-added products that conform to the Check Point Secure Virtual Network (SVN) architecture. OPSEC partners include many smaller companies as well as most of the biggest in the business— Intel, Broadcom, Nokia, Compaq, Nortel, IBM, Qwest, HP, Fujitsu, and Symantec.

Check Point's software has won numerous awards, including Product of the Year for VPN-1 from *Network Magazine* (April 2001) and Editor's Choice Awards from *Network Computing* (December 2000) and Communication News (May 2001), as well as Best Internet Infrastructure Company for 2001 from *Global Finance*.

Opportunities and Challenges

The brilliant OPSEC concept helps establish the proprietary Check Point SVN solution as the standard for network security. Other companies build solutions based on the platform, reinforcing it as the standard (in much the same way that Windows became the standard operating system). The demand for network security is growing as more and more businesses look to establish dynamic communications networks.

Gross profit margin on Check Point's software is a staggering 92.7 percent. Talk about a money-maker—that's better than Microsoft's.

The company's main challenge is to stay in the forefront of network security solutions. Check Point must continually re-invent its VPN and firewall protocols. In fact, next-generation architecture began shipping in the first quarter of 2001.

Financial Highlights

Check Point stock spiked in March 2000, when Internet mania sent everything through the roof, and took a brief dive in the two months following. Then it rose steadily to new highs, peaking in October before bouncing around and crashing in early 2001. The share price subsequently struggled to gain ground, despite a first quarter that saw revenues jump 86 percent and earnings up 141 percent year-over-year. After nearly doubling, the stock crashed to a 52-week low of US$39 on market jitters and a profit warning that the second quarter to June 30, 2001, would see revenues rise "only" 54 percent over the previous year and earnings jump "only" 88 percent. As of mid-2001, in my opinion, the stock is undervalued.

Check Point Software Technologies Ltd. at a Glance

Fiscal Year-end: December

5-Year Return: 66.1%

	1996	1997	1998	1999	2000	6-Year Growth Average (%)	6-Year Growth Total (%)
Revenue (US$ mlns.)	31.9	82.9	141.9	219.6	425.3	122.7	4,376.8
Net Income (US$ mlns.)	15.2	40.2	69.9	95.8	n/a	122.3	1,895.8
Earnings/ Share (US$)	0.07	0.18	0.30	0.39	0.84	123.8	4,100.0
Dividend/ Share (US$)	–	–	–	–	–	–	–
Price/ Earnings	31.5 - 86.3	15 - 46.8	6 - 26.5	9.8 - 95.5	34.6 - 141.2	–	–

Table data courtesy of ✓*Canadian Shareowner* **www.shareowner.com**

Stock Growth (Fiscal Year High-Low-Close)

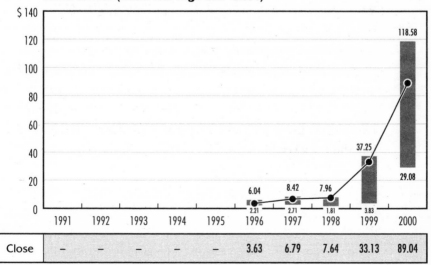

	1991	1992	1993	1994	1995	1996	1997	1998	1999	2000
Close	–	–	–	–	–	3.63	6.79	7.64	33.13	89.04

Note: Net income growth figures based on 1995–99.

EMC CORPORATION

35 Parkwood Drive
Hopkinton, MA 01748

Tel: (508) 435-1000   Employees: 24,100
www.emc.com   Founded: 1979
Symbol: EMC (NYSE)   Listed: 1986

Founder and Chairperson Emeritus: Richard J. Egan
Executive Chairperson: Michael C. Ruettgers
President and CEO: Joseph M. Tucci

Share Price Growth	★ ★ ★ ★ ★
Revenue Growth	★ ★ ★ ★ ★
EPS Growth	★ ★ ★ ★ ★
EMC	**15**

About the Company

All of the information created throughout history until 2000 consti-
tutes 12 exabytes of information. What's an exabyte? It's 1 followed
by 18 zeros bytes, or roughly the equivalent of 50,000 times the volume of the Library of Congress. That's a lot of information!

But here's the kicker: A study done by a team of researchers at the
School of Information Management and Systems at U.C. Berkeley
estimates that this will double by 2002. Two years will produce as much
information as has been produced in the preceding 300,000 years.
Stored on floppy disks it would form a stack 24 million miles high.
Really. Enter EMC Corporation, the world leader in information
storage systems.

Founded in 1979 by Richard Egan and Roger Marino (whose initials gave the company its name), EMC started as a supplier of add-on memory boards. But the company really made headway when it moved into memory systems for mainframe computers. IBM controlled 80 percent of the market, and EMC set out to create compatible but cheaper products.

In 1990 it introduced Symmetrix, intelligent information storage systems based on arrays of small disk drives and aimed at the mainframe market. In 1995 the company created the first platform-independent storage system, capable of supporting all major operating systems. EMC has also moved into the network storage area and is offering stiff competition to rival Network Appliance.

Information storage has been good to EMC. For the decade from January 1, 1990 to December 31, 1999, EMC achieved the single best decade performance of any stock in the history of the New York Stock Exchange. The stock rose an amazing 80,575 percent, or an average annual return of 95 percent.

Opportunities and Challenges

Demand for storage is expected to grow 50-fold in the next five years, according to *Fortune* magazine (October 2, 2000). *Fortune* also named EMC as one of the top three most admired companies in the world for quality of products and service. That is an unbeatable combination!

While EMC is the clear market leader, its US$8.9 billion of sales are only 20 percent of the US$50 billion market for storage, which is expected to grow to US$100 billion by 2005. EMC also has tremendous overseas potential: only 39 percent of its business is outside North America, but foreign markets represent 60 percent of worldwide IT spending.

EMC does face some competition from other sources. Computer makers such as IBM and Compaq are still major players in the storage market. And Network Appliance, the fourth-fastest growing company in America, was the dominant player in network-accessed storage

(NAS) through 2000. EMC came back strongly in the first quarter of 2001 with a product dubbed the NetApp Killer and took the lead in the NAS market away from Network Appliance. NetApp fought back by hiring away some key players on EMC's NAS team. The rivalry is getting bitter.

Even the best-performing stock of the 1990s wasn't immune to the technology debacle, and EMC shares dropped from US$102.94 in October 2000 to a low of US$25.05 in April 2001. The stock has been slow to move again, despite an excellent first quarter that saw year-over-year revenues increase 29 percent, with networked storage revenues increasing 158 percent. The company is growing in spite of lean times and is making inroads on competitors.

The second quarter of 2001 to June 30 saw the effects of the slowing economy catch up with EMC: revenues were off 5.8 percent and earnings were off 73.7 percent. Its P/E multiple at a mid-2001 price of US$18 was a very low and attractive 27. Incredibly, the price hit its lowest level since 1998. As the economy recovers, watch for EMC to regain its footing. Meanwhile, can you spell "bargoon"?

Financial Highlights

As noted, EMC nose-dived from a high of US$103 in October 2000 to a low of US$18 in mid-July 2001, and the trend was still downward at that time. Somewhere the stock will find a bottom before recovering. To its old highs? Maybe. EMC has some powerful history behind it.

EMC Corporation at a Glance

Fiscal Year-end: December

10-Year Return: 63.7%

	1996	1997	1998	1999	2000	10-Year Growth Average (%)	10-Year Growth Total (%)
Revenue (US$ mlns.)	2,273.7	2,937.9	3,973.7	6,715.6	8,872.8	52.6	3,717.9
Net Income (US$ mlns.)	386.2	538.5	793.4	1,197.8	1,782.1	86.5	13,608.5
Earnings/ Share (US$)	0.20	0.26	0.37	0.54	0.79	75.5	7,800.0
Dividend/ Share (US$)	–	–	–	–	–	–	–
Price/ Earnings	9.5 - 22.7	15.3 - 31.3	16.2 - 58.5	38.9 - 102.8	60.1 - 132.8	–	–

Table data courtesy of **✓Canadian Shareowner** **www.shareowner.com**

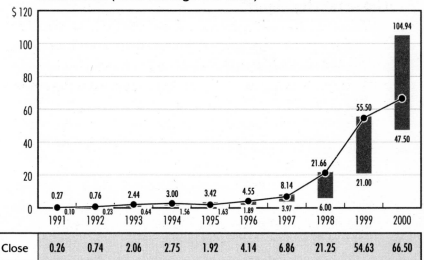

Stock Growth (Fiscal Year High-Low-Close)

Close	0.26	0.74	2.06	2.75	1.92	4.14	6.86	21.25	54.63	66.50

MERCURY INTERACTIVE CORPORATION

1325 Borregas Avenue
Sunnyvale, CA 94089

Tel: (408) 822-5200
Fax: (408) 822-5300
www.mercuryinteractive.com
Symbol: MERQ (NASDAQ)

Employees: 1,500+
Founded: 1989
Listed: 1993

President and CEO: Amnon Landan

Share Price Growth	★ ★ ★ ★ ★
Revenue Growth	★ ★ ★ ★ ★
EPS Growth	★ ★ ★ ★ ★
MERQ	**15**

About the Company

Mercury Interactive began as a company testing Windows and Unix software for corporate clients. In the late 1990s, it made a splash testing for the Y2K bug. Today Mercury tests website performance and interactive business applications for over 10,000 companies, including Amazon.com, America Online, Cisco, Citigroup, BMW, Compaq, Siemens, Verizon, Wal-Mart, and Microsoft. Even the NASDAQ uses Mercury's software to test the reliability of its trading systems and the additions of new member firms.

When Stephen King decided to go digital and offer his newest book online, he hired Mercury Interactive to make sure his website could manage the expected traffic. Mercury, in fact, has 40 percent of the software testing market.

Testing is a pretty broad term. What does Mercury do, exactly, that makes it so much in demand? As one analyst put it, Mercury provides the equivalent of an insurance policy for a company's software systems. Mercury's service solutions can test load capabilities on a website by simulating 2 million simultaneous users. Enterprise testing solutions include test management, load testing, scalability, and functional/regression testing. Clients can optimize their software and know it is working properly before it is deployed, and then monitor it 24/7 so they can correct problems quickly as they develop. And Mercury's software can fine-tune the applications as upgrades and modifications occur.

Mercury Interactive has partnered with numerous companies to make sure it can support software applications from Siebel or SAP, application servers from BEA or IBM, and databases from Microsoft or Oracle. Other alliances include Nokia, 724 Solutions, Deloitte Consulting, PriceWaterhouseCoopers, PSINet, Netscape, and Vignette.

Opportunities and Challenges

Even with the tremendous growth it has seen, business on the Internet is still in its early stages. The company was 13th of *Fortune's* 100 fastest-growing companies for 2000, number 37 on *Business Week's* 50 for 2001, number 40 on *Forbes's* "200 Best Small Companies" list, one of "Twelve Hot Companies to Watch" in *Enterprise Magazine*, and one of "Ten Tech Stocks Worth the Risk" in the May 2001 issue of *Business 2.0*.

Mercury Interactive's clientele is diversified, with only about 15 percent of its business from dot-coms. The rest are, shall we say, more stable companies. Also, Mercury has no single dominant client: In the third quarter of 2000, according to *Fortune* magazine, the company recorded 150 deals in the US$100,000 to US$750,000 range, and no deals over a million dollars.

The second quarter to June 30, 2001 saw Mercury Interactive's revenues climb 38 percent over the previous year and earnings increase 29 percent. (Earnings excluded costs associated with the company's takeover of Freshwater Software, amortization of goodwill, and one-time charges.) In a down market, this performance was exceptional.

Financial Highlights

Even after plummeting by 75 percent in the technology stock debacle of 2000–2001, the stock was still trading at a P/E ratio of over 40. Some think this is too high, but I think this fast-growing company justifies at least this multiple, and probably even higher. After bottoming around April 30, 2001, Mercury Interactive started a steady ascent, only to get beaten down again by mid-year. But its future looks solid.

Mercury Interactive Corporation at a Glance

Fiscal Year-end: December

7-Year Return: 52.7%

	1996	1997	1998	1999	2000	9-Year Growth Average (%)	9-Year Growth Total (%)
Revenue (US$ mlns.)	54.5	76.7	121.0	187.7	307.0	75.5	7,039.5
Net Income (US$ mlns.)	6.8	10.3	21.8	34.4	64.7	–	–
Earnings/ Share (US$)	0.10	0.15	0.28	0.40	0.70	–	–
Dividend/ Share (US$)	–	–	–	–	–	–	–
Price/ Earnings	23.8 - 60	15.8 - 46.9	18.9 - 56.5	26.3 - 137.8	57.3 - 232.1	–	–

Table data courtesy of www.shareowner.com

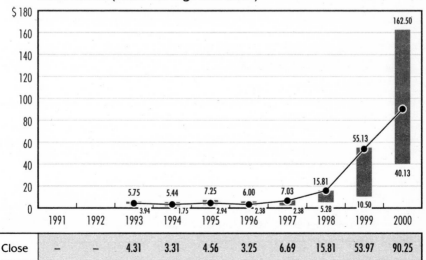

Stock Growth (Fiscal Year High-Low-Close)

	1991	1992	1993	1994	1995	1996	1997	1998	1999	2000
Close	–	–	4.31	3.31	4.56	3.25	6.69	15.81	53.97	90.25

MICROSOFT CORPORATION

One Microsoft Way
Redmond, WA 98052-6399

Tel: (425) 936-4400	Employees: 44,000
Fax: (425) 936-8000	Founded: 1975
www.microsoft.com	Listed: 1986
Symbol: MSFT (NASDAQ)	

Chairperson: William H. Gates
CEO: Steven A. Ballmer
President and COO: Rick Belluzzo

Share Price Growth	★ ★ ★ ★ ★
Revenue Growth	★ ★ ★ ★ ★
EPS Growth	★ ★ ★ ★ ★
MSFT	**15**

About the Company

Microsoft is the largest and most successful computer software company in the world and the second-largest company in America by market capitalization (after General Electric).

Founded in 1975 by Bill Gates and Paul Allen, Microsoft has come to dominate the computer software industry like a colossus. Its Windows operating system is on almost every non-Apple personal computer. Its Office software is the software of choice for business.

How successful is it? Let's look at the numbers. For the 10 fiscal years from 1991 through 2000, revenues have increased an average of

32.7 percent annually. Earnings per share have increased an average of 40.3 percent annually. An incredible record matched by few.

The company thrives on change and fosters creativity among its employees. Mr. Gates is the key architect of this success and, in my opinion, Microsoft's number-one asset. In his 1999 book, *Business @ the Speed of Thought,* he says, "in three years every product my company makes will be obsolete. The only question is whether we'll make them obsolete or somebody else will. In the next ten years, if Microsoft remains a leader, we'll have had to weather at least three major crises." Mr. Gates therefore manages Microsoft from the perspective that it's the underdog. If he doesn't, he says, "some competitor will eat our lunch."

Opportunities and Challenges

Microsoft is betting the whole ball of wax on the next phase of the Internet with its .NET initiative, launched on March 19, 2001. Basically, .NET is a user-centric set of services based on the XML language that allows people to integrate functions across different computing platforms. Instead of cluttering up your hard drive with files and programs, you'll be able to access them over the Internet. .Net lets people tailor software to themselves, rather than tailoring themselves to their software, by taking the principles of cookies and application service providers to the next level. Except that, unlike cookies, which put themselves on your computer without your consent, no one can access your data without explicit permission.

In fall 2001, Microsoft is launching Xbox—its entry into the video game business. The company will be the new kid on the block here, going toe-to-toe with Nintendo, Sega, and Sony PlayStation. This is a monster-size target market and, if successful, the product will add significantly to the company's bottom line. In October 2001, Microsoft is slated to release Windows XP, the next generation of its operating system, which will have enhanced multimedia features.

Mr. Gates expressed well the prime challenge for all businesses in the fast-changing world of computers and electronics: "One day an eager upstart will put Microsoft out of business."

The other challenge for Microsoft is the U.S. government. The antitrust hurdle could well crop up again and again for the company. Microsoft's stock took a big hit in 2000, not from the bursting tech bubble, but from the adverse antitrust ruling. However, in June 2001, an appeals court overturned the ruling that Microsoft should be split in two, though it sustained the verdict that Microsoft was guilty of monopoly practice. Microsoft has pledged to fight for total vindication.

The potential split was the most serious danger facing Microsoft, and with that soon to be behind it, the company can focus its full attention on what matters: product development and staying on the cutting edge of change.

Financial Highlights

Microsoft peaked in December 1999 before the rest of the technology market crashed, but it never took as severe a hit as some tech issues, which tanked 90 percent or more. From peak to trough, Microsoft declined about 65 percent. Since late December 2000, the stock has made a desultory comeback, and, depending on the success of Windows XP, Xbox, and .NET, could well move ahead strongly in the future.

Microsoft Corporation at a Glance

Fiscal Year-end: June
10-Year Return: 36.6%

	1997	1998	1999	2000	2001	10-Year Growth Average (%)	10-Year Growth Total (%)
Revenue (US$ mlns.)	11,358.0	14,484.0	19,747.0	22,956.0	25,296.0	20.3	817.0
Net Income (US$ mlns.)	3,439.0	4,795.3	7,582.2	9,359.2	7,346.0	32.0	937.4
Earnings/ Share (US$)	0.66	0.89	1.38	1.69	1.39	30.0	826.7
Dividend/ Share (US$)	–	–	–	–	–	–	–
Price/ Earnings	20.8 - 51.1	33.1 - 61	31.8 - 69.3	35.7 - 71	29.0 - 59.6	–	–

Table data courtesy of ✓Canadian Shareowner   www.shareowner.com

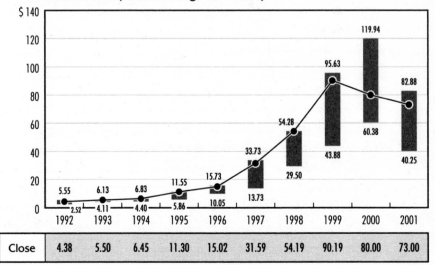

Stock Growth (Fiscal Year High-Low-Close)

| Close | 4.38 | 5.50 | 6.45 | 11.30 | 15.02 | 31.59 | 54.19 | 90.19 | 80.00 | 73.00 |

Note: Data for the year 2001 from company reports.

NETWORK APPLIANCE, INC.

495 East Java Drive
Sunnyvale, CA 94089

Tel: (408) 822-6428   Employees: 2,400
Fax: (408) 822-4412   Founded: 1992
www.netapp.com   Listed: 1995
Symbol: NTAP (NASDAQ)

CEO: Dan Warmenhoven
President: Thomas F. Mendoza

Share Price Growth	★ ★ ★ ★ ★
Revenue Growth	★ ★ ★ ★ ★
EPS Growth	★ ★ ★ ★ ★
NTAP	**15**

About the Company

The amount of data flowing across the Internet and through corporate intranets is staggering. Where do you store all that stuff? Most of it (78 percent) is still stored in computer servers and hard drives sold by the major computer manufacturers, such as IBM, Compaq, and HP. But increasingly business is turning to specialized storage systems.

The two kinds of systems have exactly opposite acronyms. Storage area networks (SANs) are large integrated systems that compete with mainframes. The leader here is EMC Corporation, which effectively stole the top spot from IBM. Network-attached storage (NAS) integrates and stores files and serves them over a network. Network Appliance is the leader in this field.

Network Appliance's servers and software solutions can integrate and store data across different platforms. For example, a company may have the computers in its accounting department running Unix and its sales department running Windows NT. Still other computers may be serving up information on the company website in HTML. Network Appliance's server can store all the data for these disparate systems in one place and make them accessible cross-platform. It does this with a specialized operating system called Data ONTAP.

The company also improves network response times with its Netcache appliance. Network caching speeds up networks by distributing content closer to end-users. Network traffic can be reduced up to 50 percent and web response time by a factor of 10, reducing what the company amusingly calls the "world wide wait." Ten of the 15 most popular websites use Network Appliance solutions.

Network Appliance has strategic partnerships with such companies as Fujitsu, Siemens, IBM Global Services, Intel, OpenWave, Oracle, RealNetworks, and SAP. The company is represented in 60 countries worldwide, with offices including a new Asia-Pacific facility in Singapore and certified support centres in Europe. Network Appliance placed fourth on 2000's Fortune 100 list of fastest-growing companies, with year-over-year growth of 70 percent over 21 quarters.

In June 2001, CEO Dan Warmenhoven was named Entrepreneur of the Year in the e-business category at Ernst & Young's annual awards banquet.

Opportunities and Challenges

Network Appliance managed to grow revenues by 13 percent for its fourth quarter to April 30, 2001, despite declining demand. This brought the company to record annual sales for fiscal 2001 of over a billion dollars U.S. As the economy recovers, sales are expected to grow at a much stronger pace.

In June 2001, the company opened a Canadian subsidiary, Network Appliance Canada. Network Appliance's Canadian presence had previously been handled by a network of partners and resellers. While many companies have been laying off employees, Network Appliance has been expanding its sales force in preparation for an economic rebound in the second half of 2001.

Rival EMC Corporation has decided to take a run at Network Appliance and grew to a 29.4 percent share of the NAS market in 2000. Each claims to offer the more cost-effective solution, but EMC is a tough and aggressive competitor and not to be underestimated. Network Appliance maintained a market share of 48.6 percent (down slightly from 49.0 percent), meaning EMC was growing at the expense of other competitors. But with the help of a secret project dubbed the NetApp Killer launched in December 2000, EMC overtook NetApp in the quarter to April 30, 2001. Rivalry between the two firms has become fierce, and in July 2001 EMC launched legal action to enforce non-competition and secrecy clauses against former employees who defected to Network Appliance. Some of the defectors (including the project leader) had worked on the NetApp Killer project.

In any event, the demand for fast-access storage is growing, and the potential market is large enough to give both companies ample room for growth. EMC is larger and has more financial clout. Network Appliance is smaller and nimbler. The outcome of this battle of the storage giants remains to be seen.

There has been criticism of the company's narrow client base—dot-coms, computer companies, and a few corporations. Part of the focus of Network Appliance's sales force expansion is to diversify its customer base.

Financial Highlights

The stock slumped badly in the backlash against tech stocks, dropping to US$10 in July 2001 from a high of US$152.75 in October 2000. Concerns over a slowing economy and competition from EMC have taken their toll. But I wouldn't count the company out yet. Watch and wait for evidence of a turnaround.

Network Appliance, Inc. at a Glance

Fiscal Year-end: April

5-Year Return: 54.1%

	1997	1998	1999	2000	2001	7-Year Growth Average (%)	7-Year Growth Total (%)
Revenue (US$ mlns.)	93.3	166.2	289.4	579.3	1,006.2	106.9	6,698.6
Net Income (US$ mlns.)	12.2	21.0	35.6	73.8	105.1	–	–
Earnings/ Share (US$)	0.04	0.07	0.12	0.21	0.29	–	–
Dividend/ Share (US$)	–	–	–	–	–	–	–
Price/ Earnings	31.3 - 93.6	25.2 - 66.7	33.3 - 139.6	46.9 - 590.5	39.4 - 526.7	–	–

Table data courtesy of Canadian Shareowner   www.shareowner.com

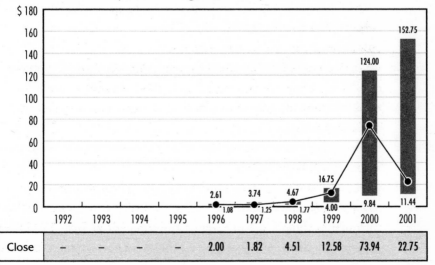

Stock Growth (Fiscal Year High-Low-Close)

	1992	1993	1994	1995	1996	1997	1998	1999	2000	2001
Close	–	–	–	–	2.00	1.82	4.51	12.58	73.94	22.75

SIEBEL SYSTEMS, INC.

2207 Bridgepointe Parkway
San Mateo, CA 94404

Tel: (650) 295-5656   Employees: 7,000+
www.siebel.com   Founded: 1993
Symbol: SEBL (NASDAQ)   Listed: 1996
        (Also SBL - TSE)

Chairperson and CEO: Thomas M. Siebel

Share Price Growth	★ ★ ★ ★ ★
Revenue Growth	★ ★ ★ ★ ★
EPS Growth	★ ★ ★ ★ ★
SEBL	**15**

About the Company

Taking advantage of the increasing popularity of the Internet as a business application, Siebel Systems has become the world's leading provider of e-business applications software, sometimes called customer relations management software (CRM).

Siebel's software enables multi-channel sales, marketing, and customer services to be applied over the Internet as well as private networks. It also supports end-user education through Siebel University, its comprehensive training program.

In 1999, Siebel Systems topped the Deloitte & Touche Fast 500 list with an incredible five-year revenue growth of 782,978 percent. That's no misprint. Siebel also topped the *Fortune* list of the fastest-growing companies that year. In 2000 it came in third on the *Fortune* list and was named the most influential software company by *Business Week*, beating out Microsoft.

Siebel was not, however, the only CRM company in the market. Canada's Janna Systems made the Canadian Fast 50 from 1998 to 2000 and was one of Canada's best-performing stocks. Janna merged with Siebel in November 2000, resulting in exchangeable shares of Siebel becoming available on the Toronto Stock Exchange.

Siebel has 144 offices in 38 countries worldwide. Its client list includes such notables as IBM, Microsoft, Charles Schwab, Yahoo!, Chase Manhattan Bank, Kellogg's, and Deutsche Telecom.

Opportunities and Challenges

In spite of the popularity of the Internet and computer networks, the industry is still in its infancy. Opportunities for growth, particularly in business services, remain plentiful, although the pace of growth will undoubtedly slow from its blistering performance of the last few years. Acquisitions such as the Janna merger should keep Siebel in the forefront of the CRM business. Sales are already topping US$2 billion a year.

In April 2001, the company announced a new line of software— employee relationship management (ERM)—expanding its market reach beyond its CRM offerings. CIBC World Markets says that U.S. companies spend US$160 billion annually on hiring, training, managing, and retaining employees.

Siebel's management is top-notch. Tom Siebel was recognized by *Business Week* in January 2001 as one of the top 25 managers in the world. He has extensive experience in the business, having served in executive positions with both Oracle and Sybase before founding Siebel Systems in 1993.

However, Siebel is not without competition. Oracle, the second-largest software company in the world, after Microsoft, has taken aim at the CRM market with its own Oracle11i suite. And in 1999, PeopleSoft acquired Vantive, the number-two CRM company, as a basis for the creation of its PeopleSoft 8 CRM software. German software giant SAP has also entered the market with its mySAP CRM line. Those are strong competitors, and Siebel faces a real challenge in staying top dog in this field.

The first quarter to March 30, 2001, saw Siebel continue its blistering pace of growth, with revenues up 87 percent and EPS climbing 114 percent year-over-year. But the second quarter saw revenue growth drop to 38 percent while earnings growth dropped to 56 percent, as the slowing economy started to have an effect.

Financial Highlights

Siebel recovered quickly from the first wave of the technology rout in March 2000, reaching new highs in early November, but then overvaluation caught up with it and the stock plummeted from US$120 to US$25. Revenue and earnings growth are clearly starting to slow for Siebel, but at least there is still growth and not retreat. As the economy recovers, look for the company to accelerate again.

Siebel Systems, Inc. at a Glance

Fiscal Year-end: December

4-Year Return: 92.8%

	1996	1997	1998	1999	2000	6-Year Growth Average (%)	6-Year Growth Total (%)
Revenue (US$ mlns.)	39.2	118.8	391.5	790.9	1,795.4	209.8	22,342.5
Net Income (US$ mlns.)	5.1	20.3	56.1	122.1	164.3	428.7	54,666.7
Earnings/ Share (US$)	0.02	0.07	0.14	0.27	0.31	–	–
Dividend/ Share (US$)	–	–	–	–	–	–	–
Price/ Earnings	69.5 - 189.1	23.7 - 88.2	27 - 66.1	29.2 - 170.4	105.6 - 386.7	–	–

Table data courtesy of ✓Canadian Shareowner   www.shareowner.com

Stock Growth (Fiscal Year High-Low-Close)

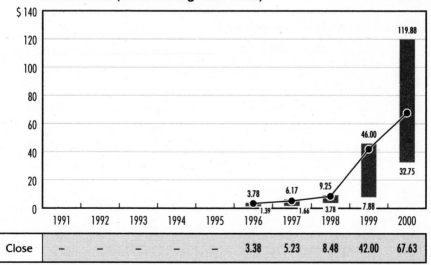

	1991	1992	1993	1994	1995	1996	1997	1998	1999	2000
Close	–	–	–	–	–	3.38	5.23	8.48	42.00	67.63

SOLECTRON CORPORATION

847 Gibraltar Drive
Milpitas, CA 95035

Tel: (408) 956-6542   Employees: 65,000
Fax: (408) 956-6059   Founded: 1977
www.solectron.com   Listed: 1986
Symbol: SLR (NYSE)

Chairperson, President, and CEO: Koichi Nishimura

Share Price Growth	★ ★ ★ ★ ★
Revenue Growth	★ ★ ★ ★ ★
EPS Growth	★ ★ ★ ★ ★
SLR	**15**

About the Company

Biggest doesn't always mean best, but in Solectron's case it just might. Solectron is the world's largest electronics manufacturing services (EMS) company, with annual sales in 2000 of over US$14 billion. Forty thousand employees working in 20 manufacturing plants around the world put together circuit boards, cellphones, servers, computer workstations, notebooks, pagers, routers, modems, NICs, printers, fax machines, airplane avionics systems—you name it.

The company has built a solid reputation in the outsourcing business for its quality work and attention to the customer. Solectron prides itself on customer service and has twice won the prestigious Malcolm Baldrige National Quality Award administered by the National Institute of Standards and Technology. This award was established in 1987 to recognize and foster quality and productivity in U.S. enterprise, which was seen to be lagging behind foreign competitors in dedication to quality. Solectron was the first company to win the Baldrige Award twice in the 13-year history of the program. It's interesting to note, too, that the stocks of companies that have won the Baldrige Award have outperformed the S&P 500 by better than 4 to 1 since 1995.

The company has also won 250 other quality and service awards. Clients include such giants as Cisco Systems, Ericsson, IBM, Hewlett-Packard, and Nortel Networks.

Solectron placed 73rd on the Fortune 100 list of the fastest-growing companies in the U.S. for 2000.

Opportunities and Challenges

Contract manufacturing is on the rise throughout the world as companies strive to compete more effectively. In fact, independent industry analysts predict that the EMS industry will grow at 28.5 percent a year until 2004.

One-third of all electronics are produced in Japan—a key target market. Solectron set up an office in Tokyo in the early 1990s and has successfully solicited business there for years. Company CEO Koichi Nishimura is of Japanese heritage and speaks the language fluently.

Solectron has been growing by acquisition as well as internally, and 2000 saw it buy up selected plants from Nortel in California and Ontario as well as plants from Ericsson, Alcatel, and IBM.

While Solectron has certainly been growing revenues at an incredible rate—65.8 percent in 2000—it did not grow as fast as some of its smaller rivals that year. Sanmina sales grew 220 percent, Singapore's Flextronics' revenues gained 140 percent, and Canada's Celestica was up 84.2 percent. These rivals, particularly Celestica, which already does two-thirds the business of Solectron, could close the gap and take over its market leadership.

Contract manufacturing is a very competitive business, so pressures on margins will continue. Nevertheless, Merrill Lynch analyst

Jerry Labowitz thinks Solectron will have no trouble hitting sales of US$30 billion or US$40 billion in a few years.

Financial Highlights

After climbing steadily from US$10 in 1998 to US$47 in January 2000, Solectron traded in a wide range from US$30 to US$47 through most of 2000 before succumbing to the tail-end of the technology wipeout—dropping to US$15 in July 2001. Revenues for the quarter ending May 31, 2001, were up 9.3 percent year-over-year, but down 26.5 percent from the previous quarter. The company also suffered a loss of 28 cents a share. The worldwide economic slowdown is having a negative effect.

Solectron Corporation at a Glance

Fiscal Year-end: August

10-Year Return: 43.8%

	1996	1997	1998	1999	2000	10-Year Growth Average (%)	10-Year Growth Total (%)
Revenue (US$ mlns.)	2,817.2	3,694.4	5,288.3	8,391.4	14,137.5	57.0	5,226.9
Net Income (US$ mlns.)	114.2	171.8	198.8	293.9	522.6	56.6	4,877.1
Earnings/ Share (US$)	0.27	0.35	0.41	0.57	0.84	38.7	1,580.0
Dividend/ Share (US$)	–	–	–	–	–	–	–
Price/ Earnings	13.4 - 23.4	12.2 - 32.5	17.6 - 32.8	17 - 69.2	33.6 - 58.9	–	–

Table data courtesy of **www.shareowner.com**

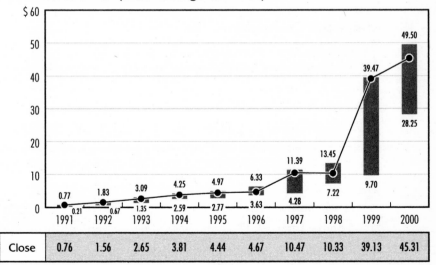

Stock Growth (Fiscal Year High-Low-Close)

	1991	1992	1993	1994	1995	1996	1997	1998	1999	2000
Close	0.76	1.56	2.65	3.81	4.44	4.67	10.47	10.33	39.13	45.31

YAHOO! INC.

701 First Avenue
Sunnyvale, CA 94089

Tel: (408) 349-3300
www.yahoo.com/investor
Symbol: YHOO (NASDAQ)

Employees: 3,259
Founded: 1994
Listed: 1996

Chairperson and CEO: Terry Semel
President and COO: Jeffrey Mallett

Share Price Growth		★ ★ ★ ★ ★
Revenue Growth		★ ★ ★ ★ ★
EPS Growth		★ ★ ★ ★ ★
YHOO		**15**

About the Company

Do you Yaho-oo-oo-oo-oo? That's the question on the company's TV and theatre commercials. And it's a rallying cry that has brought over 190 million unique users a month to the collection of websites known as Yahoo!

Jerry Yang and David Filo, two graduate students in electrical engineering at Stanford, created Yahoo! as a directory to the fledgling and growing Internet in 1994. Something like a library catalogue system, Yahoo! led the user quickly to information on virtually any topic.

Today Yahoo! is the most highly trafficked and most-recognized brand on the Internet. From its superb finance pages to auctions to movies to personal websites, Yahoo! keeps people coming back for more. Over a billion page views were generated in March 2001. Yahoo! has the most loyal audience on the Internet, with a 77.5 percent retention rate. And in February 2001 it was the number-one default home page, with 35.5 million users—41.4 percent of all users—according to Media Metrix.

Yahoo! has made a name for itself in messaging; Yahoo! Messenger, Yahoo! Mail, and Yahoo! Groups delivered over 10 billion messages in March 2001. Not quite up to the U.S. Postal Service yet, but getting there.

Business services and advertising bring in most of the company's revenues, which amounted to over a billion dollars U.S. in 2000.

Opportunities and Challenges

Yahoo! early in its life sought out top-notch management, who turned the company into the powerhouse it is today. Tim Koogle, named one of the top 25 executives for 1999 by *Business Week*, headed the company from 1995, growing it from startup to billion-dollar company.

In May 2001, the company appointed Terry Semel to the position of chairperson and CEO. Previously, Mr. Semel was the chairperson and co-CEO of Warner Brothers, where he was instrumental in building the company from one revenue stream and US$1 billion a year in sales, to multiple revenue streams and US$11 billion. He led the company to 18 consecutive years of record revenues and profits. His experience in multimedia and the motion picture industry will benefit Yahoo! as media convergence accelerates.

Yahoo! stock got clobbered in the tech wreck. From a high of US$250, the stock plunged to US$11, a 95 percent drop. While this may sound scary, this low level represents an unprecedented opportunity to get into a world-class company with terrific growth potential at prices not seen since July 1998. However, the bursting of the Internet stock bubble affected not only Yahoo!'s prices but also revenues. First-quarter predictions for the balance of 2001 forecast revenues between US$700 million and US$775 million, down considerably from 2000. Earnings are expected to break even.

The challenge for Yahoo! is to build on its strengths and grow despite any weaknesses in the economy. The acquisition of Terry Semel as chairperson and CEO should play a major role in achieving this.

Financial Highlights

After plunging from US$250 in January 2000 to US$11 in April 2001, the stock found a trading range between US$15 and US$23. In a few years this level of pricing will be seen for the bargain it is.

Yahoo! Inc. at a Glance

Fiscal Year-end: December
5-Year Return: 50.7%

	1996	1997	1998	1999	2000	6-Year Growth Average (%)	6-Year Growth Total (%)
Revenue (US$ mlns.)	19.1	67.4	203.3	588.6	1,110.2	406.5	79,200.0
Net Income (US$ mlns.)	-2.3	1.7	37.0	114.4	90.2	–	–
Earnings/ Share (US$)	-0.01	0.01	0.08	0.19	0.15	–	–
Dividend/ Share (US$)	–	–	–	–	–	–	–
Price/ Earnings	-129.2 - -358.3	139.6 - 887.5	90 - 893.8	289.5 - 1178.9	167.1 - 1667.1	–	–

Table data courtesy of  **✓Canadian Shareowner** **www.shareowner.com**

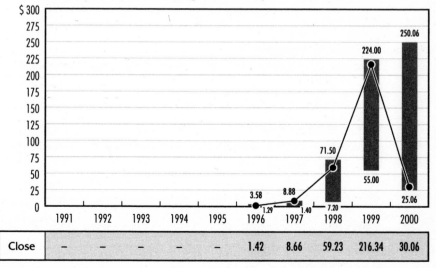

Stock Growth (Fiscal Year High-Low-Close)

	1991	1992	1993	1994	1995	1996	1997	1998	1999	2000
Close	–	–	–	–	–	1.42	8.66	59.23	216.34	30.06

INTEL CORPORATION

2200 Mission College Blvd.
PO Box 58119
Santa Clara, CA 95052-8119

Tel: (408) 765-8080   Employees: 86,100
www.intel.com   Founded: 1968
Symbol: INTC (NASDAQ)   Listed: 1971

Chairperson: Andrew S. Grove
President and CEO: Craig R. Barrett

Share Price Growth	★ ★ ★ ★ ★
Revenue Growth	★ ★ ★ ★
EPS Growth	★ ★ ★ ★ ★
INTC	**14**

About the Company

Faster than a speeding bullet! More powerful than a locomotive! Able to leap tall buildings in a single bound! Well, not really the last two. But Intel Labs has developed a new transistor just 20 nanometres in size. By around 2007 this should enable the creation of microprocessors with a billion transistors running at speeds approaching 20 gigahertz at less than one volt.

How fast is that? Faster than a speeding bullet! This future microprocessor will be able to do four million calculations in the time it takes a bullet to travel one inch. A billion calculations in the blink of an eye. Each transistor switch will be able to turn on and off more than a trillion times a second.

Intel co-founder Gordon Moore coined a maxim in 1965 called Moore's Law: The number of transistors that can be put in an integrated circuit will double every 18 months. He expected this rate of growth to last until 1975, but it remains true today and, with the development of the tiny transistor noted above, will hold for another 10 years.

Mr. Moore and Robert Noyce, co-inventor of the integrated circuit, left industry pioneer Fairchild Semiconductor to found Intel in 1968. Together with 10 others, they developed the company into the powerhouse it is today. The story is long and elaborate, but suffice to say that integrated circuits led to microprocessors which led to the revolution of the personal computer.

The 6,000 scientists working in Intel's 80 research labs worldwide are not creating planned obsolescence, but planned progress. The world of computing is constantly getting faster, smaller, and more powerful, and Intel is in the forefront of these developments. You've probably got a little blue "Intel Inside" label on your computer— Intel's microprocessors are inside 85 percent of the world's personal computers.

Revenues in 2000 topped US$33 billion. To give you an idea of what a phenomenal investment Intel has been over the years, US$1,000 invested when it first went public 30 years ago would be worth over US$1.5 million today. Although Intel's core business is still microprocessors for computers, it also produces components for wireless devices—mobile phones, PDAs, and so on—and it builds chips for networking—embedded circuits for hubs, routers, switches, and servers.

Opportunities and Challenges

Although the clear industry leader, Intel is not without competition. Applied Micro Devices (AMD), maker of the Duron and Athlon microprocessors, has been gaining ground and is no slouch. Nevertheless, Intel, with its size and clout, not to mention its US$4 billion a year R&D budget, should meet and beat the competition.

Revenues for the first quarter to March 31, 2001 were off 16 percent, with earnings off 63 percent, but the company still turned a profit. The second quarter to June 30, 2001 saw earnings plunge 76 percent, but this had already been factored into the stock price, and the quarter met analyst expectations. Slowing computer sales, a faltering economy, and strong price competition from AMD all took their toll.

Financial Highlights

Intel shares suffered with the rest of the technology market, declining from a high of US$75.81 in September 2000 to a low of US$22.25 in April 2001, before settling into a trading range between US$25 and US$35. Increased efficiencies, new products in the pipe, and a recovering economy make Intel a bargain today at prices not seen since 1999.

Intel Corporation at a Glance

Fiscal Year-end: December
10-Year Return: 31.8%

	1996	1997	1998	1999	2000	10-Year Growth Average (%)	10-Year Growth Total (%)
Revenue (US$ mlns.)	20,847.0	25,070.0	26,273.0	29,389.0	33,726.0	25.0	605.8
Net Income (US$ mlns.)	5,157.0	6,945.0	6,218.6	7,587.9	9,205.1	33.9	1,024.5
Earnings/ Share (US$)	0.72	0.97	0.88	1.09	1.32	33.2	1,000.0
Dividend/ Share (US$)*	0.02	0.03	0.03	0.05	0.07	3.0	600.0
Price/ Earnings	8.6 - 24.1	16.4 - 26.3	18.7 - 35.8	23 - 41.1	22.6 - 57.4	–	–

Table data courtesy of ✓Canadian Shareowner   www.shareowner.com

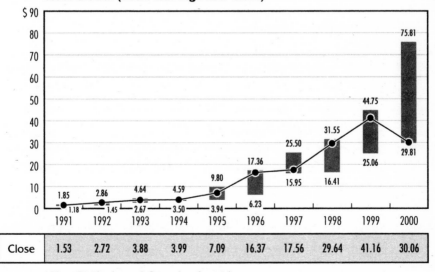

Stock Growth (Fiscal Year High-Low-Close)

	1991	1992	1993	1994	1995	1996	1997	1998	1999	2000
Close	1.53	2.72	3.88	3.99	7.09	16.37	17.56	29.64	41.16	30.06

High/Low values shown: 1.85/1.18, 2.86/1.45, 4.64/2.67, 4.59/3.50, 9.80/3.94, 17.36/6.23, 25.50/15.95, 31.55/16.41, 44.75/25.06, 75.81/29.81

* Note: Dividend growth figures based on eight years.

COGNOS INC.

3755 Riverside Drive
Ottawa, ON K1G 4K9

Tel: (613) 738-1440   Employees: 2,500
Fax: (613) 738-0002   Founded: 1969
www.cognos.com   Listed: 1986
Symbol: CSN (TSE) (Also COGN-NASDAQ)

President and CEO: Renato Zambonini

Share Price Growth	★ ★ ★ ★ ★
Revenue Growth	★ ★ ★
EPS Growth	★ ★ ★ ★ ★
CSN	**13**

About the Company

When the NASDAQ wanted to coordinate its comprehensive data to provide a useful analytical tool on its website, who did it turn to? When NASA was looking for a way to coordinate information on 20,000 employees working out of nine different field centres, who did it turn to? If you answered Cognos, you're right.

Ottawa-based Cognos is the world's largest and most successful business intelligence company. Its suite of software products operate on its Enterprise Business Intelligence (EBI) Platform to allow companies to coordinate and creatively use company data. These uses range from predictive modelling, financial reporting, budgeting, forecasting, analysis, and queries, to scenario creation and visualization.

The EBI Platform is not so much a product as an infrastructure that supports the manipulation of corporate data. Its applications vary from customer to customer.

Cognos's data platform incorporates the Internet to enable easy data sharing between various geographical operations of an organization. E-business solutions are also part of the company's activities.

More than 2.4 million Cognos Business Intelligence licences have been sold to over 17,000 organizations in over 120 countries. These include such major companies as Nielsen Data Research, ABN AMRO Bank, BMW, Mercedes-Benz, Dow Chemical, Shell Oil, Nokia, Hewlett-Packard, Philips, Hydro Quebec, Bertelsmann Music Group, Siemens, and KLM.

Opportunities and Challenges

In late 2000, Cognos entered the corporate portal market with its Enterprise Portal Partner (EPP) program. A portal program, such as the Plumtree Corporate Portal, integrates data from various programs and platforms into one customized common user interface or desktop. Cognos's EPP program enlists portal providers as partners to integrate Cognos's business intelligence software into their offerings. As of late January 2001, it had already signed on five corporate portal providers (including Plumtree) to integrate its program to enhance their offerings. Business analyst Summit Strategies estimates the portal market will reach US$14 billion by 2002, and business intelligence is seen as a killer app in this market.

Cognos also has a number of strategic alliances with companies whose products, together with Cognos's EBI solutions, complement and enhance each other. These include Microsoft, PeopleSoft, Siebel, and SAP.

Everybody's bogeyman, the economy, is also Cognos's bugbear. The company announced a 10 percent cut in its workforce just before releasing its quarterly report to May 31, 2001. Revenues for the quarter were flat and earnings plunged into the red, showing a 13 cent loss per share compared to EPS of 14 cents the year before. On the up-side, CEO Ron Zambonini announced in April 2001 that Cognos will take advantage of fallen share prices to acquire some small, complementary companies. Cognos had cash reserves of US$239 million in mid-June.

Financial Highlights

Cognos shares soared from $15 in October 1999 to a high of $73 in November 2000, before falling in the second wave of the tech wreck to $24 in April 2001. After regaining some ground, the stock hit a new 52-week low of $22 in mid-2001 and may go lower before the company, along with the economy, finds its footing again.

Cognos Inc. at a Glance

Fiscal Year-end: February

10-Year Return: 24.8%

	1997	1998	1999	2000	2001	10-Year Growth Average (%)	10-Year Growth Total (%)
Revenue ($ mlns.)	270.9	348.6	454.4	559.4	759.4	20.8	423.0
Net Income ($ mlns.)	51.1	72.2	92.8	85.3	101.0	–	1,842.3
Earnings/ Share ($)	0.56	0.79	1.04	0.97	1.10	–	1,471.4
Dividend/ Share ($)	–	–	–	–	–	–	–
Price/ Earnings	19.6 - 47.8	15.8 - 31	10.9 - 20.8	14.7 - 55.7	23 - 66.5	–	–

Table data courtesy of **www.shareowner.com**

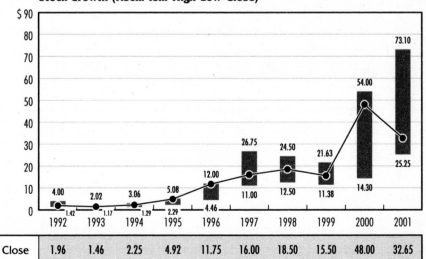

Stock Growth (Fiscal Year High-Low-Close)

	1992	1993	1994	1995	1996	1997	1998	1999	2000	2001
Close	1.96	1.46	2.25	4.92	11.75	16.00	18.50	15.50	48.00	32.65

THQ INC.

27001 Agoura Road, Suite 325
Calabasas Hills, CA 91301

Tel: (818) 871-5000   Employees: 410
www.thq.com   Founded: 1989
Symbol: THQI (NASDAQ)   Listed: 1991

Chairperson, President, and CEO: Brian J. Farrell

Share Price Growth	★ ★ ★
Revenue Growth	★ ★ ★ ★ ★
EPS Growth	★ ★ ★ ★ ★
THQI	**13**

About the Company

Is there a North American home with kids that doesn't have a video game system? I don't know of any, and moreover, everyone wants the latest thing. When the PlayStation 2 came out in October 2000, people lined up for 26 hours outside one store in San Francisco.

Whatever game system a kid may have, the slot in the game console is like a hungry mouth demanding more and better games. Enter THQ, the fourth-largest publisher of electronic games.

The company covers all current platforms: Game Boy, Game Boy Color, Nintendo 64, PlayStation, PlayStation 2, Sega Dreamcast, and computer games for Windows and Macintosh. And THQ is building games for the systems to be launched in fall 2001: Microsoft's Xbox, Nintendo GameCube, and Nintendo Game Boy Advance.

THQ makes dozens of games—some developed in-house and many licensed. Its licences include the extremely popular WWF series, which had brought in over US$190 million as of March 2001. WWF SmackDown 2 was the number-one seller for 11 out of 12 weeks in the first quarter of 2001. WWF No Mercy topped the charts in its first week, and three more WWF games are in the pipe.

Other licences include popular series for younger children: Rugrats, Scooby-Doo, Hot Wheels, Power Rangers, Star Wars, and Disney Interactive, as well as several properties from Nickelodeon. THQ dominates this juvenile market with a 37 percent market share, more than double that of the next publisher.

THQ was the 17th fastest-growing company in America, according to the Fortune 100 list published in September 2000.

Opportunities and Challenges

Credit Suisse/First Boston initiated coverage of three game makers, including THQ, on May 1, 2001. Analyst Heath Terry said, "We believe that the interactive entertainment industry is just beginning what will be the largest and most significant growth phase in its history."

The next wave of video game consoles is due to hit the store shelves in fall 2001, and it will hit with a vengeance. Each succeeding generation of game technology outsells its predecessor. Eight-bit games sold 30 million units, 16-bit games sold 36 million, 32- and 64-bit games sold 45 million, and the next-generation games are forecast to sell 65 million units. THQ has 25 titles ready for these systems.

Wireless and online technology present new opportunities. THQ is working with Siemens to develop games for mobile devices. WWF: With Authority, a game hosted on the WWF website, was released in February 2001. And THQ's video-intensive games are being readied for broadband release as the technology becomes available.

THQ is growing its market share of the video game market—7.0 percent in 2000, up from 5.2 percent in 1999—while most of its rivals are losing share. However, one competitor has moved up even faster: Activision jumped from a 3.8 percent share in 1999 to a 7.7 percent share in 2000.

Gross profit margins are substantial for all video game makers and could lead to some price competition, but most people buy games based on content, not price. THQ's biggest challenge is to keep developing innovative games that appeal to the kid in all of us.

THQ's 10-year history did not meet our criteria for inclusion, as the company lost money in 1993 and 1994 before undergoing a dramatic reorganization in 1995, including a one-for-15 share consolidation. Our analysis (including star ratings) is based on the company's fortunes since 1994. The share prices in the data have been adjusted for this consolidation, which explains their high value in the early 1990s. So if the star ratings and some of the data in our tables don't match, that is why. Specifically, from its low point in 1994 to 2000, revenues grew from US$13.3 million to US$347.0 million, up 2,509.0 percent. Earnings per share grew from US$0.08 to US$1.65, an increase of 1,962.5 percent, and share price climbed from US$4.17 to US$24.38, a jump of 484.7 percent.

Financial Highlights

Since June 1995, THQ has risen from a low of US$0.67 to a high of US$62.00 on June 29, 2001. Although it did suffer some fallout from the technology crash, dropping from US$38 in November 1999 to US$10 in June 2000, it has risen in an almost straight line since November 2000 through July 2001, a period during which many technology stocks suffered significant downturns.

THQ Inc. at a Glance

Fiscal Year-end: December

9-Year Return: 2.9%

	1996	1997	1998	1999	2000	10-Year Growth Average (%)	10-Year Growth Total (%)
Revenue (US$ mlns.)	50.3	89.4	215.1	302.4	347.0	49.8	954.7
Net Income (US$ mlns.)	1.9	9.3	23.3	36.9	35.6	–	768.3
Earnings/ Share (US$)	0.17	0.60	1.33	1.83	1.65	–	-25.0
Dividend/ Share (US$)	–	–	–	–	–	–	–
Price/ Earnings	8.3 - 28.1	4.3 - 17.5	4.8 - 15.7	6 - 21.4	4.6 - 18.2	–	–

Table data courtesy of ✓**Canadian Shareowner** **www.shareowner.com**

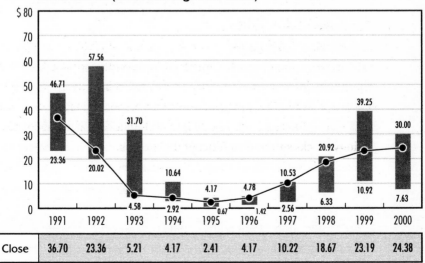

Stock Growth (Fiscal Year High-Low-Close)

Close	36.70	23.36	5.21	4.17	2.41	4.17	10.22	18.67	23.19	24.38
	1991	1992	1993	1994	1995	1996	1997	1998	1999	2000

SAPIENT CORPORATION

One Memorial Drive
Cambridge, MA 02142

Tel: (617) 621-0200
Fax: (617) 621-1300
www.sapient.com
Symbol: SAPE (NASDAQ)

Employees: 2,600
Founded: 1991
Listed: 1996

Co-Chairperson and Co-CEO: Jerry A. Greenberg
Co-Chairperson and Co-CEO: J. Stuart Moore

Share Price Growth	★ ★
Revenue Growth	★ ★ ★ ★ ★
EPS Growth	★ ★ ★ ★
SAPE	**11**

About the Company

Sapient, according to the Oxford Dictionary, means "wise" or "of or relating to the human species." Luckily, the company lives up to both meanings of its marvellous name.

What's the wise idea behind Sapient? Founders Stuart Moore and Jerry Greenberg noted that the problem with most business consultancies was that contracted projects often came in late and over budget. Why not create a business and technology consultancy based on good service? What a concept!

So the duo maxed out eight credit cards to get the business going in 1991. Sapient's upfront commitment to a fixed price and fixed delivery time caught on with customers, and revenues grew to over US$500 million in 2000.

Today the company employs 2,600 people, creating business, technology, and Internet solutions for industries as varied as energy, financial services, industry, retail, transportation, and communications. Sapient also has strategic alliances with big-name vendors such as Microsoft, Oracle, Siebel, Sun, and IBM, among others, to implement solutions for clients. Clients include American Airlines, Avon, Chevron, Dell, ESPN, Hallmark, Lloyd's of London, McDonald's, Nissan, Nokia, Pepsi, Procter & Gamble, SC Johnson, Shell, Texaco, Unilever, Wal-Mart, and the U.S. Marine Corps.

Sapient was the 32nd fastest-growing company in America in 2000 according to *Fortune* magazine, and one of 10 featured as "the best of the bunch." This growth was all internally financed: The company is debt-free and has ample cash reserves.

Sapient has offices in 18 cities around the world, including four in Europe and two in Asia. It opened a Canadian office in March 2001 headed by Linda Lizotte-MacPherson, the former chief information officer for the Government of Canada, who led the government's Y2K program.

Opportunities and Challenges

With today's emphasis on cost control and tight budgets, Sapient's fixed-price, fixed-delivery policy is likely to become even more popular with companies looking to implement new technology. The company is particularly focused on increasing its Asian presence.

Sapient couldn't escape the slowing economy, however, and took serious steps to restructure in the first quarter of 2001, closing its Sydney, Australia, office and laying off 720 people, or about 20 percent of its workforce. The focus was on retaining its skill-sets, but reorganizing around the services most in demand. In May 2001 the company announced its first quarterly loss since going public, despite a 9 percent increase in revenues. Slower growth and restructuring were the primary reasons.

Despite its superior service, Sapient is still relatively unknown. The major challenge for the company, aside from weathering the down economy, is to leverage its success to further its expansion into foreign and domestic markets.

Financial Highlights

Sapient hit a peak of US$74.50 in August 2000 before crashing and burning to slightly north of US$5 in early April 2001. A rally to US$14 fizzled and the stock entered a trading range between US$6 and US$10 in mid-2001.

Sapient Corporation at a Glance

Fiscal Year-end: December

5-Year Return: 8.9%

	1996	1997	1998	1999	2000	6-Year Growth Average (%)	6-Year Growth Total (%)
Revenue (US$ mlns.)	44.6	90.4	160.4	276.8	503.3	87.6	2,198.2
Net Income (US$ mlns.)	6.6	12.7	20.8	31.8	47.0	78.0	1,578.6
Earnings/ Share (US$)	0.07	0.12	0.19	0.25	0.35	55.3	775.0
Dividend/ Share (US$)	–	–	–	–	–	–	–
Price/ Earnings	52.2 - 104	31.3 - 65.4	31.9 - 90.8	47.8 - 282.5	25.5 - 216	–	–

Table data courtesy of **Canadian Shareowner   www.shareowner.com**

Stock Growth (Fiscal Year High-Low-Close)

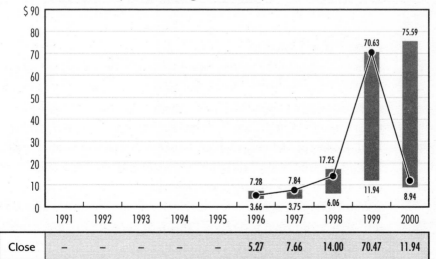

	1991	1992	1993	1994	1995	1996	1997	1998	1999	2000
Close	–	–	–	–	–	5.27	7.66	14.00	70.47	11.94

ATI TECHNOLOGIES INC.

33 Commerce Valley Drive East
Thornhill, ON L3T 7N6

Tel: (905) 882-2600	Employees: 1,976
Fax: (905) 882-2620	Founded: 1985
www.ati.com	Listed: 1993
Symbol: ATY (TSE) (Also ATYT-NASDAQ)	

CEO: K. Y. Ho
President and COO: Dave Orton

Share Price Growth	★ ★ ★ ★ ★
Revenue Growth	★ ★ ★ ★
EPS Growth	0
ATY	**9**

About the Company

Although some folks may pooh-pooh the old Horatio Alger rags-to-riches stories, the story of Kwok Yuen Ho could be one. Mr. Ho grew up in the 1950s in mainland China, where he peddled vegetables from the garden to help the family finances. His father worked in Hong Kong, eking out a living and sending money home. Eventually Mr. Ho, his parents, and a brother were re-united in Hong Kong where they lived together in a tiny one-room flat.

Mr. Ho went on to study electrical engineering at a Taiwanese university, and then progressed through a number of electronics companies in Hong Kong. In 1983 he immigrated to Canada where, two years later, he and two friends started Array Technologies Inc., operating out of a garage. They specialized in graphics cards for PCs, primarily for hobbyists. By 1993, when ATI went public, graphics cards were a must-have item, and the company was pulling down annual sales of $221 million.

ATI Technologies is now the world's largest manufacturer of 3D graphics and multimedia technology. Its products are installed as standard equipment on computers made by the major manufacturers. ATI's brand names include Rage, Xpert, All-in-Wonder, and Radeon. The company also makes video capture cards so you can tune in television on your PC.

In 1998 Mr. Ho was named Canada's Entrepreneur of the Year. The following year *Business Week* named him as one of the Top 25 business executives in the world, along with such luminaries as Jurgen Schrempp of Daimler Benz, Michael Dell of Dell Computers, Craig Barrett of Intel, and Steve Jobs of Apple Computers. The poor kid who sold vegetables is now a much-honoured multimillionaire. Now that's a real-life Horatio Alger story!

Opportunities and Challenges

ATI Technologies fell on hard times in 2000, despite sales increasing by 9.6 percent to over $2 billion. Profits were halved, and the stock price dropped from a high of $33.60 to $5.60.

However, the company is expanding into the game console business; its technology is the power behind Nintendo's soon-to-be-released GameCube.

In 1998, ATI's leading rivals in the computer graphics field were Diamond and Matrox, both of whom fell by the wayside, but nVidia came roaring up the middle and now has 48 percent of the desktop PC market to ATI's 33 percent. ATI still leads in laptops, with 57 percent of the market. ATI's cross-licensing agreements with Intel could give it an edge over nVidia with new products coming onstream, and ATI's products also have a price advantage.

The market may settle out, with ATI maintaining dominance in the portable market and nVidia in desktops. Or one company could become king of the hill and swallow up the other. Time and the market will tell.

As noted in our Introduction, the fact that ATI's one allowable year of losses came in 2000 gave it a negative earnings growth for the entire period. The company is expected to return to profitability in 2002.

Financial Highlights

ATI was the Canadian wonder stock of 1997 and 1998, climbing from $5 to a high of $27 in January 1999. Growth slowed in 2000 as profit turned to substantial loss, the first in the company's history. The stock stumbled back to $6 by March 2001. But narrowing losses and the prospect of returning to profitability in 2002 have seen the stock on a tear since then.

ATI Technologies Inc. at a Glance

Fiscal Year-end: August

7-Year Return: 19.2%

	1996	1997	1998	1999	2000	8-Year Growth Average (%)	8-Year Growth Total (%)
Revenue ($ mlns.)	466.6	602.8	1,156.9	1,842.7	2,019.8	39.9	811.1
Net Income ($ mlns.)	27.3	47.7	168.4	204.4	-111.9	91.5	-4,244.4
Earnings/ Share ($)*	0.14	0.24	0.79	0.92	-0.52	94.4	-2,700.0
Dividend/ Share ($)	–	–	–	–	–	–	–
Price/ Earnings	14.5 - 23	11.1 - 24.5	7.4 - 25.6	12.2 - 30.3	-21.9 - -64.6	–	–

Table data courtesy of ✓*Canadian Shareowner* **www.shareowner.com**

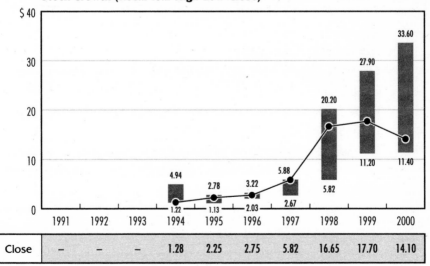

Stock Growth (Fiscal Year High-Low-Close)

Close	–	–	–	1.28	2.25	2.75	5.82	16.65	17.70	14.10

* Note: EPS growth figures based on seven years.

CELESTICA INC.

844 Don Mills Road
Toronto, ON M3C 1V7

Tel: (416) 448-2211   Employees: 31,000
Fax: (416) 448-2280   Founded: 1994
www.celestica.ca   Listed: 1998
Symbol: CLS (TSE) (Also NYSE)

Chairperson and CEO: Eugene V. Polistuk
President and COO: J. Marvin MaGee

Share Price Growth	★ ★ ★
Revenue Growth	★ ★ ★
EPS Growth	★ ★ ★
CLS	**9**

About the Company

Celestica is a young company, founded in January 1994 as the wholly owned manufacturing arm of IBM. In October 1996, Gerald Schwartz's Onex Corporation bought the company, importing IBM management to run it.

Eugene Polistuk, a 25-year veteran with IBM Canada, was Celestica's president and CEO from inception and steered the company through its transformation from IBM subsidiary to its current position as the third-largest electronics manufacturing services (EMS) company in the world. That evolution saw it grow from two facilities in two countries with 2,500 employees in 1996 to 36 plants in 34 countries and

31,000 employees in 2001. In July of 1998, Celestica went public, with the largest technology IPO in Canadian history.

Celestica's client structure has also changed dramatically in its short life. In 1997, 77 percent of its business was with IBM. Today it has a diversified customer base that includes such giants as Cisco, Nortel, HP, Sun Microsystems, Dell, EMC, NEC, Motorola, JDS Uniphase, Lucent, Nokia, and Juniper Networks.

Celestica provides a wide range of services, including design, pro-totyping, assembly, testing, supply chain management, distribution, and after-sales service for original equipment manufacturers. The company's commitment to excellence and investment in state-of-the-art facilities, including the world's most advanced inspection tech-nology, has created strong working relationships with its clients. The company is also competitive in cost management.

In June 2001, Celestica topped the list in *Business Week*'s Information Technology 100, the best info tech companies in the world. The emerg-ing theme of the list? Efficiency rules!

Opportunities and Challenges

Despite the tech stock crash in 2000 and 2001, the Internet and re-lated technologies are still in their infancy and will recover. Celestica has set an ambitious target of $30 billion in sales by 2003, double its 2000 revenue of $14.6 billion. The company's revenues for the first quarter of 2001 were up 67 percent over the previous year, and earn-ings were up 95 percent. But revenue growth dropped off to 27 per-cent in the second quarter, with profits excluding goodwill up 36.7 percent. The company also announced further staff cuts.

Some critics fear that Celestica may lose its number-one client, IBM, putting a big dent in its operations. IBM and Sun Microsystems are the company's two leading customers, each accounting for over 10 percent of revenues. But the company's ability to forge into new areas and attract new customers, including such dynamic companies as Juniper Networks, Agilent, and EMC, show it to be on the right track.

As an electronics manufacturing services company, though, Celestica's health is dependent on the health of its customers. Some, such as Lucent, are looking rather shaky. But others, such as Juniper Networks, are exceptionally strong. A diversified base of over 75 customers has helped.

The challenges facing the electronics industry will drive more and more OEMs to contract out manufacturing to companies such as Celestica to cut costs. So the problems facing the sector may actually be beneficial for EMS providers.

Financial Highlights

From a peak of $128 in October 2000, Celestica stock dropped 70 percent to a low of $38 in April 2001. The stock recovered significantly to settle in a trading range between $60 and $80 in mid-2001.

Celestica Inc. at a Glance

Fiscal Year-end: December

2-Year Return: 61.0%

	1996	1997	1998	1999	2000	4-Year Growth Average (%)	4-Year Growth Total (%)
Revenue ($ mlns.)	–	2,866.6	4,995.7	7,649.4	14,623.0	72.9	410.1
Net Income ($ mlns.)	–	11.8	-11.8	105.2	335.3	9.3	2,741.5
Earnings/ Share ($)	–	0.34	-0.12	0.63	1.54	4.6	352.9
Dividend/ Share ($)	–	–	–	–	–	–	–
Price/ Earnings	–	–	-66.7 - -176	29.2 - 131.6	33.1 - 83.3	–	–

Table data courtesy of **Canadian Shareowner** **www.shareowner.com**

Stock Growth (Fiscal Year High-Low-Close)

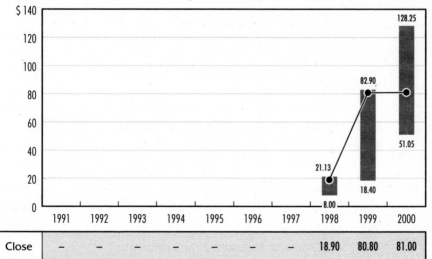

Close	–	–	–	–	–	–	–	18.90	80.80	81.00

INTERNET SECURITY SYSTEMS, INC.

6303 Barfield Road
Atlanta, GA 30328

Tel: (404) 236-2943   Employees: 1,500
Fax: (404) 236-2626   Founded: 1994
www.iss.net   Listed: 1998
Symbol: ISSX (NASDAQ)

President and CEO: Thomas E. Noonan
Chief Technology Officer: Christopher W. Klaus

Share Price Growth	★ ★
Revenue Growth	★ ★ ★ ★ ★
EPS Growth	★
ISSX	**8**

About the Company

When Bill Gates suggested that Microsoft could be put out of business by a company not yet started, with a product not yet invented by some kid in high school, he could have been thinking of Christopher Klaus.

Mr. Klaus was just a senior in high school in 1991 when he invented a new technology for identifying and fixing network security weaknesses. A year later, as a 19-year-old computer science student at the Georgia Institute of Technology, he released his invention, called Internet Scanner, as freeware on the Internet.

In 1994, he founded Internet Security Systems with Tom Noonan, a former senior manager at Dunn & Bradstreet Software, as president and CEO. With Mr. Klaus's technical savvy and Mr. Noonan's business expertise, ISS became one of the fastest-growing companies in the United States, hitting fifth on the Deloitte & Touche Fast 500 list for the year 2000.

ISS products go way beyond simple virus detection. They actively assess, identify, and correct weaknesses, including analyzing user privileges, file system access rights, and inadequate password protection (even advising if a password is too easy to guess). The company says its products aim to "stop hackers, crackers and cyber-thieves cold."

Its SAFEsuite platform of security products is so sought after that its clientele includes 21 of the 25 largest U.S. commercial banks, 10 of the largest telecommunications companies, 35 government agencies, including the U.S. Army, and the aforementioned Microsoft. ISS also offers managed security—it monitors and manages a client's security 24/7 from its Security Operations Centre, as home security companies do with burglar alarm systems. In fact, Mr. Noonan says, "We want to be the ADT of the Internet."

Internet Security Systems employs 1,500 people in 17 countries. In an industry in which employee turnover averages 20 percent, the company's employees are incredibly loyal and dedicated—turnover is only 2 percent.

In 1999, Mr. Klaus was honoured by MIT's *Technology Review* magazine as one of the Top 100 innovators in America. In March 2001, International Data Corporation named ISS as the worldwide leader in Intrusion Detection and Vulnerability Assessment.

Opportunities and Challenges

Security is a necessity for any company doing business on the Internet, so ISS has only scratched the surface of its potential market, even if that surface includes most of the major banks. Its client base is just

8,000. The challenge for ISS is to grow its market share in the Internet security business.

The company has numerous strategic alliances with companies such as Microsoft, Nortel, Compaq, Check Point, and BellSouth. One of the more interesting is the alliance with Marsh, one of the world's leading risk advisors and insurance brokers. ISS assesses and remediates security problems to help clients qualify for insurance coverage.

In spite of its impressive client list and many awards, ISS is still a relatively unknown company. Revenues are still under US$250 million a year as of the first quarter of 2001. But revenues for the first quarter to March 31, 2001, showed strong year-to-year revenue growth of 56 percent, with earnings more than doubled.

The economy caught up with ISS in the second quarter, when revenue growth slowed to 17 percent and it posted a pro forma loss of 2 cents a share. Several large potential sales had been reduced or delayed. The company announced some restructuring to realize cost efficiencies and lowered its projections for the balance of 2001. Nevertheless, the revised projections still call for a 35 percent revenue increase over 2000.

Financial Highlights

ISS hit a peak of US$140 in March 2000, then crashed like all the other Internet stocks, hitting a low of US$20 in April 2001. After surging back to US$60 after the first quarter of 2001, the stock plunged back to the US$20 level after the second quarter results. The stock can be volatile. Most of that plunge occurred in one day on July 3, 2001, as the stock dropped from US$50.17 to US$29.99—a 40 percent drop. It could go lower before finding a bottom, but long-term prospects look good.

Internet Security Systems, Inc. at a Glance

Fiscal Year-end: December

3-Year Return: 37.0%

	1996	1997	1998	1999	2000	5-Year Growth Average (%)	5-Year Growth Total (%)
Revenue (US$ mlns.)	4.5	13.5	35.9	116.5	195.0	165.1	4,233.3
Net Income (US$ mlns.)	-1.1	-3.9	-3.3	8.6	18.3	–	–
Earnings/ Share (US$)	-0.14	-0.50	-0.11	0.20	0.41	–	–
Dividend/ Share (US$)	–	–	–	–	–	–	–
Price/ Earnings	–	–	-77.3 - -275.6	100 - 355.6	112.8 - 343.9	–	–

Table data courtesy of www.shareowner.com

Stock Growth (Fiscal Year High-Low-Close)

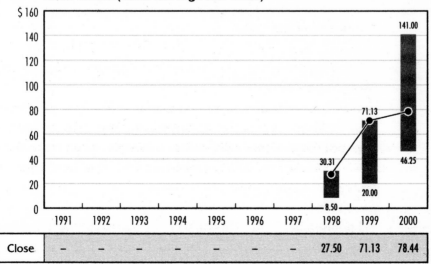

THE THOMSON CORPORATION

TD Bank Tower, Suite 2706
Toronto, ON M5K 1A1

Tel: (416) 360-8700	Employees: 47,800
Fax: (416) 360-8812	Founded: 1934
www.thomson.com	Listed: 1965
Symbol: TOC (TSE)	

Chairperson: Kenneth R. Thomson
President and CEO: Richard J. Harrington

Share Price Growth	★ ★
Revenue Growth	★
EPS Growth	★
TOC	**4**

About the Company

Until the year 2000, the Thomson Corporation was one of the world's great newspaper organizations. But, perhaps signifying the importance of the Internet and electronic information systems, not to mention Thomson's foresight, the company sold off all its newspaper holdings lock, stock, and barrel in 2000 to focus on electronic information services.

Thomson began in 1934 when family patriarch Roy Thomson bought his first newspaper in Timmins, Ontario. In 1953 he bought his first British paper, and the following year moved to Scotland to start his international empire. He already owned more newspapers in Canada than any other company. By 1964, when Thomson was honoured by being named Lord Thomson of Fleet, he had television stations, newspapers, and business and consumer magazines in his stable.

Thomson Newspapers Limited went public in Canada in 1965. By the time he died in 1976, Lord Thomson had been involved in travel companies, an airline, and North Sea oil exploration, but information was always his first love.

After some reorganization, the company had major interests in specialized information publishing and electronic database services. This was the future as the company saw it—the British newspapers were sold in 1995, and Thomson Travel in 1998.

The year 2000 saw the company transformed in to a giant of the information age in nothing short of a flurry of activity. Sold: all the community newspapers in North America. Acquired: 40 companies, including Prometric, Wave Technologies, Dialog, IOB of Brazil, Carson Group, Primark, La Ley in Argentina, Greenhaven Books, and Lucent Press. All are involved in technical, legal, and financial publishing or in electronic information systems.

Finally, in 2001, Thomson bit the bullet and sold its flagship darling, the *Globe and Mail*, to Bell Globemedia, in which it holds a 20 percent interest.

The company's vision is nothing less than "to be the world's foremost global e-information and solutions company in the business and professional marketplace."

Lord Thomson's vision made his family the richest in Canada, with an estimated net worth of US$16.1 billion (according to *Forbes*'s 2000 list), four times as much as the runner-up Irvings of New Brunswick. Ken Thomson's vision may repeat this feat in the electronic information age.

Opportunities and Challenges

The specialized information field is large and lucrative, and Thomson has moved aggressively to control it. In the legal field it owns Westlaw, Sweet & Maxwell, Thomson & Thomson, Carswell, and other respected brands with operations around the world. 2000 Revenues: US$2.6 billion.

In the financial arena, everyone has heard of Thomson/First Call, but the company also owns such brands as Baseline, Datastream International, digiTrade, and MarketEye. 2000 Revenues: US$1.3 billion.

Thomson also has electronic databases and information systems for the scientific and health care fields, and education, including corporate training. The Education Division includes such well-known reference book publishers as Charles Scribner's Sons, Macmillan, Nelson, and Wadsworth.

With the increasing importance of information to business, the scientific community and education, Thomson has a firm foothold in a very rich market. The biggest challenges facing the company now are to integrate all its newly acquired assets and to proceed with further global expansion.

Chairperson Kenneth Thomson retires in 2002, when his son David will take over. It remains to be seen if he can adequately fill his father's shoes.

Thomson is not a go-go stock that is going to make a big splash, but it will not crash and burn like many more volatile stocks either. This is a blue chip company for the information age.

Financial Highlights

Thomson stock has been on a steady uptrend since mid-1994, with occasional corrections. It peaked on October 2000 at $64 before meandering back to $50, a decline of only 22 percent, a mild setback compared to other technology stocks. From its chart, this setback is, as of mid-July 2001, within the parameters of its long-term uptrend.

The Thomson Corporation at a Glance

Fiscal Year-end: December
10-Year Return: 15.9%

	1996	1997	1998	1999	2000	10-Year Growth Average (%)	Total (%)
Revenue ($ mlns.)	10,578.0	12,522.9	9,638.7	8,306.1	9,767.6	5.7	51.2
Net Income ($ mlns.)	568.6	764.2	783.8	667.5	698.0	9.8	106.8
Earnings/ Share ($)	0.95	1.26	1.28	1.08	1.12	8.2	83.6
Dividend/ Share ($)	0.76	0.81	0.94	0.98	1.02	7.8	96.2
Price/ Earnings	19.5 - 32.9	20.8 - 32.1	22.7 - 35.9	32.9 - 47.2	33 - 57.6	–	–

Table data courtesy of Canadian Shareowner www.shareowner.com

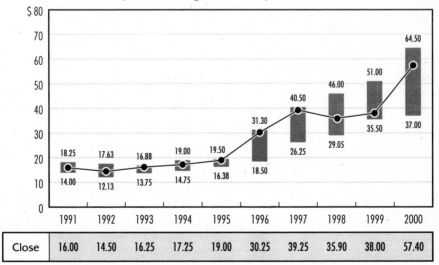

Stock Growth (Fiscal Year High-Low-Close)

	1991	1992	1993	1994	1995	1996	1997	1998	1999	2000
Close	16.00	14.50	16.25	17.25	19.00	30.25	39.25	35.90	38.00	57.40

TELECOMMUNICATIONS

Aastra Technologies Ltd.
C-Mac Industries Inc.
Comverse Technology Inc.
PMC-Sierra, Inc.
Research in Motion Ltd.
Wescam Inc.
BCE Inc.

AASTRA TECHNOLOGIES LTD.

155 Snow Boulevard
Concord, ON L4K 4N9

Tel: (905) 760-4200	Employees: 115
Fax: (905) 760-4233	Founded: 1991
www.aastra.com	Listed: 1998
Symbol: AAH (TSE)	

Chairperson and CEO: Francis Shen
President and COO: Anthony Shen

Share Price Growth	★ ★ ★ ★ ★
Revenue Growth	★ ★ ★ ★ ★
EPS Growth	★ ★ ★ ★ ★
AAH	**15**

About the Company

Aastra Technologies makes telephones. Sounds like a simple enough business, and perhaps that's why it has been so successful. Aastra specializes in developing and distributing home telecom equipment including telephones, handsets, caller ID adjuncts, and Internet-enabled phones.

In 1999 and again in 2000, the company made the Deloitte & Touche Technology Fast 50 list as one of the fastest-growing companies in Canada. Revenues had exploded from $3.2 million in 1994 to $97 million in 1999. The company accelerated this feat in 2000 when revenues doubled again to $188.7 million, and should make the Fast 50 for the third consecutive year in September 2001. *Profit Magazine*'s Profit 100 for 2001 has already been published, and Aastra came in as the 19th fastest-growing company in Canada, with a 4,415 percent jump in revenues from 1995 to 2000.

Aastra has managed such stellar growth by focusing on certain classes and types of products and by avoiding butting heads with such giants as Sony, GE, and Panasonic. Its products include a number of industry firsts, such as the first integrated caller ID telephones, the first cordless phone with caller ID, and the first ADSI (analog display services interface) compatible phone.

In December of 1999, Aastra purchased some of Nortel Networks' telephone manufacturing assets, including over 20 design patents and numerous trademarks such as Vista, PowerTouch, Nomad, Maestro, and Symphony. It also has the exclusive licence to market telephone products under the Bell trademark, serving all the major North American telcos, most of which also carry the Bell name. This is a huge franchise.

Seventy-five percent of Aastra's sales are exported to the U.S., with the rest in Canada. Its products are sold through all major North American telephone companies, as well as through retailers such as Radio Shack and Wal-Mart.

On April 20, 2001, Aastra was added to the TSE 300 Composite Index.

Opportunities and Challenges

In November 2000 Aastra took over Global ADSI Solutions (GLADSIS). Global's technology allows the transmission of both voice and data simultaneously over screen phones. This merger of telephony and Internet services, including e-mail, could be a very popular feature in a few years, since it gives Internet access to non-PC users. (Can Dick Tracy's wrist phone be far behind?)

In May 2001, Aastra acquired more of Nortel's assets, its Meridian Business Sets, Centrex, and ISDN terminal interests. The acquisition includes manufacturing tools, equipment, patents, contracts, and inventory. Again, these assets will facilitate convergence of telephony and digital information. Telephony is changing, and Aastra is on the cutting-edge of these changes, which should bode well for the future.

The biggest challenge facing Aastra (and many other companies as well) is the economy. Sales for the first quarter of 2001 to March 31 were down 6 percent, though improved margins helped increase profits by 51 percent.

The company's acquisition spree saw it issue $55 million in special warrants in January 2000, resulting in a dilution of earnings per share. First quarter EPS increased only marginally, from $0.30 in 2000 to $0.31 in 2001, in spite of the growth in profits. But Aastra did launch a normal course issuer bid late in 2000 to repurchase up to 5 percent of its shares.

Aastra Technologies is one of the stocks that did not meet all our qualifications, because it had losses for 1996 and 1997. However, it has been profitable every year since, and earnings more than doubled from 1998 to 1999 and again to 2000.

Financial Highlights

Aastra stock exploded from October 1999 to March 2000, jumping from $5 to $17. The stock then fell to $8 by October 2000. But, unlike many technology stocks that underwent a second stage of decline to April 2001, Aastra actually went up from December 2000 to the end of May. Aastra started sliding a bit towards mid-year, but if sales growth can be recaptured, the stock should continue its ascent.

Aastra Technologies Ltd. at a Glance

Fiscal Year-end: December

3-Year Return: 106.5%

	1996	1997	1998	1999	2000	8-Year Growth Average (%)	8-Year Growth Total (%)
Revenue ($ mlns.)	6.7	13.1	37.2	97.1	188.7	101.2	10,640.9
Net Income ($ mlns.)	-0.2	-0.4	1.3	5.2	17.2	–	71,566.7
Earnings/ Share ($)	-0.03	-0.05	0.16	0.51	1.26	–	12,500.0
Dividend/ Share ($)	–	–	–	–	–	–	–
Price/ Earnings	-1.6 - -25	-1.3 - -32.7	3.8 - 21.9	6.4 - 30.2	4 - 13.9	–	–

Table data courtesy of ✓*Canadian Shareowner* **www.shareowner.com**

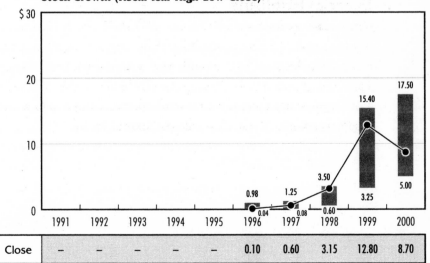

Stock Growth (Fiscal Year High-Low-Close)

| Close | – | – | – | – | – | 0.10 | 0.60 | 3.15 | 12.80 | 8.70 |

Note: Data for the years 1993–97 from company reports.

C-MAC INDUSTRIES INC.

1010 Sherbrooke Street West, Suite 1610
Montreal, QC H3A 2R7

Tel: (514) 282-7629	Employees: 10,000
Fax: (514) 282-3402	Founded: 1985
www.cmac.com	Listed: 1992
Symbol: CMS (TSE) (Also EMS-NYSE)	

Chairperson, President, and CEO: Dennis Wood

Share Price Growth	★ ★ ★ ★ ★
Revenue Growth	★ ★ ★ ★ ★
EPS Growth	★ ★ ★ ★ ★
CMS	**15**

About the Company

Montreal-based C-MAC Industries is an international designer and manufacturer of electronic components and full systems for a range of industries, including communications, transportation, and aerospace. It operates 52 manufacturing facilities, primarily in North America and Europe, but also in India and China. These plants are supported by eight design centres in North America and Europe.

The company started out focused on the communications industry but now encompasses six divisions: Engineering, Network Systems, Electronic Systems, Micro-technology, Automotive, and Energy.

C-MAC has grown quickly in recent years, through both internal growth and acquisition. In 2000 its acquisitions included the Invotronics division of Magna International; Kavlico Corporation, the world's largest independent supplier of precision sensors; DY4 Systems, a leader in digital signal processing and products for harsh environments; and a number of business units from Nortel Networks. In January 2001 it acquired a plant in Florida and another in Mexico from Honeywell.

The focus of C-MAC's acquisitions has been selective vertical integration as well as expanding its manufacturing capabilities. Indeed, revenue for 2000 was more than double that in 1999.

Opportunities and Challenges

The company's acquisition strategy has added depth and value to the company's offerings to original equipment manufacturers. As the trend to outsourcing continues, C-MAC is in an excellent position to profit from these investments.

The company's research facilities have also created proprietary manufacturing processes and technologies that enable the production of highly specialized, complex products and that shave costs for clients. C-MAC's goal is to differentiate itself with technologies designed to reduce time to market. The company spent $41.46 million on research in 2000, about 1.6 percent of sales.

Profit margins for contract manufacturers are often stretched thin in the competition for business. C-MAC's gross profit margin has been eroding steadily over the last five years, to 17.2 percent in 2000. Nevertheless, C-MAC boasts the highest gross margins in the electronics outsourcing industry. Its small size relative to giants such as Celestica or Solectron gives it an edge, and also makes the company a possible takeover target down the road.

A more serious challenge for C-MAC is its reliance on Nortel Networks as a primary customer. C-MAC is the main assembler for optical communications equipment for Nortel. Nortel, in fact, contributed 66 percent of revenues for C-MAC at one point, but this has been reduced to 42 percent as of April 2001. That's still a hefty chunk of C-MAC's business, and the company's fortunes could ride in synch with Nortel's to some extent. C-MAC has managed to diversify, and its automotive components business is growing apace.

I've included C-MAC in the Telecommunications section because of its heavy focus on that area, but it could just as easily have been included in the Industry or Information Technology sections. C-MAC reported a superior first quarter to March 31, 2001, with revenues up 75 percent and earnings before goodwill amortization also up 75 percent year-over-year. Gross profit margin was up as well. The second quarter saw growth continue in spite of Nortel, albeit at a slower pace, with revenues up 32 percent and earnings before goodwill amortization up 41 percent. However, share dilution resulted in EPS being up only 15 percent.

Financial Highlights

The company lost over 70 percent of its market value in the technology rout. Although expectations have been trimmed with the downturn in the telecom market, C-MAC is still growing, though not at the blistering pace of the nine years to 2001.

Late Breaking News: On August 9, 2001, it was announced that C-MAC is merging with Solectron (another of our 50 Best). The deal is to be completed by the end of 2001, so C-MAC may no longer be available as a public company by the time you read this. Exchangeable shares of Solectron on the TSE may be in the offing, but that was not confirmed at press time.

C-MAC Industries Inc. at a Glance

Fiscal Year-end: December

8-Year Return: 36.8%

	1996	1997	1998	1999	2000	9-Year Growth Average (%)	9-Year Growth Total (%)
Revenue ($ mlns.)	318.0	414.3	645.5	1,174.6	2,552.8	50.8	2,083.7
Net Income ($ mlns.)	14.7	20.3	25.4	45.2	132.8	59.4	1,975.0
Earnings/ Share ($)	0.29	0.40	0.49	0.76	1.74	50.1	1,238.5
Dividend/ Share ($)	–	–	–	–	–	–	–
Price/ Earnings	7.1 - 17	11.7 - 28.8	15.1 - 32.7	14.7 - 58.2	18.9 - 65.2	–	–

Table data courtesy of ✓*Canadian Shareowner* **www.shareowner.com**

Stock Growth (Fiscal Year High-Low-Close)

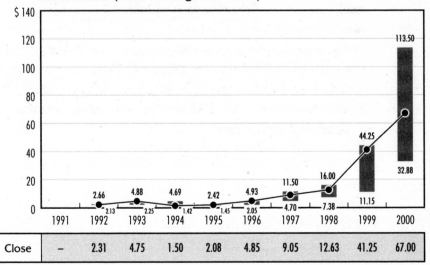

	1991	1992	1993	1994	1995	1996	1997	1998	1999	2000
Close	–	2.31	4.75	1.50	2.08	4.85	9.05	12.63	41.25	67.00

COMVERSE
TECHNOLOGY INC.

170 Crossways Park Drive
Woodbury, NY 11797

Tel: (516) 677-7200   Employees: 6,000
Fax: (516) 677-7355   Founded: 1984
www.cmvt.com   Listed: 1986
Symbol: CMVT (NASDAQ)

Chairperson and CEO: Kobi Alexander

Share Price Growth	★ ★ ★ ★ ★
Revenue Growth	★ ★ ★ ★ ★
EPS Growth	★ ★ ★ ★ ★
CMVT	**15**

About the Company

In two words—voice mail. Comverse does it so well that it is the world's leading provider of software and systems for messaging systems. The company operates three main business divisions: Comverse Network Systems, Comverse Infosys, and Ulticom.

The top dog, generating 84 percent of revenues, is Comverse Network Systems. It supplies unified messaging services for major telecoms around the world. If you use your telephone company's call answer service, voice messaging system, or even fax, e-mail, or video messaging services, chances are you are using Comverse technology.

And, of course, there are corporate networks—we all hate calling up a company and getting those annoying "If you want Accounting, push 1, if you want Sales, push 2, if you want the president of the company, hang up and don't try again later" messages. Nevertheless, Comverse sells a lot of these systems.

Comverse Infosys is in the business intelligence, customer relations management, and monitoring fields. That includes digital recording and monitoring systems used by government and law enforcement agencies. Yes—if the Mounties are tapping your phone, they may be doing it with help from Comverse.

Ulticom is involved in intelligent network services. Even though it generates only 4 percent of the company's revenues, Ulticom's services are ubiquitous, deployed by over 250 carriers in 90 countries serving 80 percent of the world's population. Network services include global roaming for cell phones, prepaid calling, calling cards, Internet call waiting, and a host of others.

Comverse is truly a giant in its field, with revenues exploding from US$15.8 million in fiscal 1991 to US$1,225.1 million in fiscal 2001.

Opportunities and Challenges

As telecoms push into the global marketplace, Comverse is right there offering services to enhance revenue. In fact, 64 percent of Comverse's sales are generated outside the U.S. and Canada. In May 2001, Comverse was selected as the exclusive provider of short messaging systems and voice mail in China.

The company's services cover all carrier systems from wireline to wireless, local networks to the Internet. It is prepared for convergence as the world moves to broadband applications such as streaming video services and picture messaging. When video stores start supplying movies for download over phonelines, Comverse will be there with the systems to make it happen. There's a lot of future potential here.

With over a billion dollars a year in revenue, some analysts think Comverse is reaching saturation and is overvalued with a P/E over 40. But its target market is much bigger than a billion dollars. After all, Microsoft sold US$15 billion in 1998, and didn't everybody have a computer by then? Well, Microsoft pulled in US$23 billion in 2000. It ain't too big until the fat company sings!

Financial Highlights

Comverse weathered the tech downturn in 2000 fairly well, dropping from US$120 to US$70, and then climbing back to new highs in January 2001. Then the roof caved in and the stock plummeted to US$45. The stock started a desultory climb back up again in April 2001.

Comverse Technology Inc. at a Glance

Fiscal Year-end: January

10-Year Return: 42.6%

	1996	1997	1999	2000	2001	10-Year Growth Average (%)	10-Year Growth Total (%)
Revenue (US$ mlns.)	197.2	280.3	696.1	872.2	1,225.1	60.3	5,706.2
Net Income (US$ mlns.)	30.0	43.5	111.5	191.6	279.5	76.9	11,080.0
Earnings/ Share (US$)	0.38	0.54	0.78	1.08	1.47	43.8	2000.0
Dividend/ Share (US$)	–	–	–	–	–	–	–
Price/ Earnings	14.1 - 36.7	19.4 - 33.9	12.6 - 36.6	20.1 - 73.4	42.2 - 84.9	–	–

Table data courtesy of ✓*Canadian Shareowner* **www.shareowner.com**

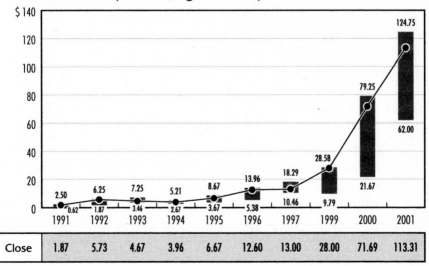

Stock Growth (Fiscal Year High-Low-Close)

Close	1.87	5.73	4.67	3.96	6.67	12.60	13.00	28.00	71.69	113.31

Note: Beginning in fiscal 1999, the company's fiscal year-end changed from December to January. January 1998 is not included in these data.

PMC-SIERRA, INC.

105-8555 Baxter Place
Burnaby, BC V5A 4V7

Tel: (604) 415-6144
Fax: (408) 988-8276
www.pmc-sierra.com
Symbol: PMCS (NASDAQ)

Employees: 1,726
Founded: 1984
Listed: 1991

Chairperson, President, and CEO: Robert L. Bailey

Share Price Growth	★ ★ ★ ★ ★
Revenue Growth	★ ★ ★ ★ ★
EPS Growth	★ ★ ★ ★ ★
PMCS	**15**

About the Company

The future of the communications revolution is broadband—the ability to transfer huge amounts of data using various protocols over the same infrastructure pipeline. PMC-Sierra is at the technological forefront of that revolution, as one of the leading designers of high-speed, high-density, broadband semiconductor architecture for asynchronous transfer mode, Internet protocol, T1/E1, and T3/E3, among other applications.

A transfer protocol is the method by which data are transferred, whether by wire, fibre optics, or wireless. For example, Internet protocol (IP) is the way data are encoded for transfer over the Internet.

You may have heard the term "IP address," the addressing system by which data find their way to the right computer (so that a website you click to finds its way to your computer and not your neighbour's). Bank machines use a different protocol, as do the credit card verification systems used by retail stores.

Founded in 1984, PMC-Sierra really got going in 1993 after it recruited Bob Bailey, who had previously turned around AT&T's moribund Microelectronics Semiconductor division. The following year he forged a merger between privately held PMC-Sierra and Sierra Semiconductor.

Focusing on research and development of the chip sets that go into networks, the company moved ahead steadily from revenues of US$8 million in 1993 to US$694 million in 2000.

PMC-Sierra is fabless, meaning it doesn't manufacture its own products, concentrating instead on design. The company was, in fact, the sixth-largest R&D spender in Canada in 2000, with a budget of over $200 million.

PMC-Sierra is a co-founder of the Saturn Development Group, a consortium of over 30 companies that works to establish networking standards, and a member of over a dozen other industry associations. The Saturn Group makes sure current and future equipment designed or manufactured by members work together seamlessly.

Over 100 customers include the who's who of networking companies—Nortel, Cisco, Lucent, Alcatel, and many more. The two largest customers, Cisco and Lucent, each account for over 10 percent of PMC-Sierra's revenues.

Mr. Bailey's leadership led to the company winning the Kachina Award for the Best Financially Managed Fabless Semiconductor Company in 1998. It won a similar award in 1999. And in 2000, Mr. Bailey was named CEO of the Year by *Electronic Business* and one of the Top Ten CEOs of 2000 by *Investor's Business Daily*.

Opportunities and Challenges

The world is going broadband, and demand for faster and better-integrated networking equipment to handle the traffic will materialize of necessity, in spite of the strong slowdown in demand in late 2000 and early 2001.

As a fabless company, PMC-Sierra has weathered the downturn better than many of its customers and competitors. It forged ahead with research and development and released 16 new products in the first quarter of 2001. In June 2001 it released its new RM9000x2 single-chip multiprocessor, said to set a new standard for high-speed networking. The product will be used in routers as well as enterprise servers. Routers handle all the complex switching operations that get data from one place to another and form an integral part of the Internet's backbone.

The economy is still a big question mark for many. PMC-Sierra logged its first quarterly operational loss for the second quarter to June 30, 2001. There may be a few more before the bloodletting is finished. But the company is well positioned for a turnaround in the networking market, being flush with cash and without long-term debt.

Although headquartered in Canada and regarded as one of Canada's leading companies, PMC-Sierra is legally a U.S. company registered in Delaware, and trades on the NASDAQ. It is regarded as foreign content in RRSP portfolios, which presents one more good argument for scrapping the Canadian content requirement.

Financial Highlights

PMC-Sierra stock, like most companies in the networking business, took a beating in the tech wreck, declining from US$246.25 to US$18.66. The stock likely will trade in a range from US$20 to US$40 until demand for networking gear picks up again.

PMC-Sierra, Inc. at a Glance

Fiscal Year-end: December
10-Year Return: 29.9%

	1996	1997	1998	1999	2000	10-Year Growth Average (%)	10-Year Growth Total (%)
Revenue (US$ mlns.)	188.4	127.2	161.8	262.5	694.7	35.9	708.7
Net Income (US$ mlns.)	2.1	33.3	40.6	90.6	124.8	1,490.4	860.0
Earnings/ Share (US$)	0.02	0.26	0.32	0.60	0.69	–	331.3
Dividend/ Share (US$)	–	–	–	–	–	–	–
Price/ Earnings	98.4 - 309.4	13.3 - 33.8	17.9 - 51.3	26.1 - 134.3	87 - 370.3	–	–

Table data courtesy of **www.shareowner.com**

Stock Growth (Fiscal Year High-Low-Close)

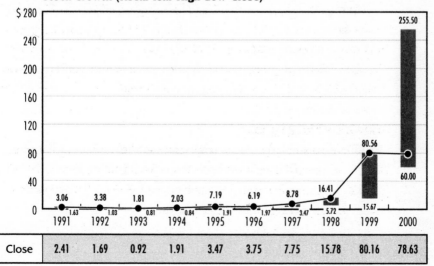

| Close | 2.41 | 1.69 | 0.92 | 1.91 | 3.47 | 3.75 | 7.75 | 15.78 | 80.16 | 78.63 |

RESEARCH IN MOTION LTD.

295 Phillip Street
Waterloo, ON N2L 3W8

Tel: (519) 888-7465   Employees: 800+
Fax: (519) 888-7884   Founded: 1984
www.rim.net   Listed: 1997
Symbol: RIM (TSE) (Also RIMM-NASDAQ)

Chairperson and Co-CEO: Jim Balsillie
President and Co-CEO: Mike Lazaridis

Share Price Growth	★ ★ ★ ★
Revenue Growth	★ ★ ★ ★ ★
EPS Growth	★ ★ ★ ★ ★
RIM	**14**

About the Company

Waiting at the podium, Al's fingers fly across the tiny keyboard of his BlackBerry pager as he types, "I'm in the middle of debate prep. Paul [his verbal sparring partner] is talking. They're wondering what I'm doing."

His wife's message comes back quickly: "Oh, I know what I'd like to be doing with you right now [lascivious comment deleted]."

"I'm losing my concentration now," Al answers. "We have to stop."

(And you thought there would be no sex in a book on stocks!)

The above conversation between presidential candidate Al Gore and wife Tipper was one of many exchanges between the couple on their BlackBerry pagers, according to Associated Press reporter

Sandra Sobieraj (Newsweek, November 20, 2000). The Democratic candidate, his wife, and a dozen aides used the little devices made by Waterloo's Research in Motion extensively during the campaign.

The BlackBerry has won numerous awards as well as the accolades of *Business Week, c/net, Forbes, Fortune, Information Week, Internet Week, PC Computing, Wired,* and others. Comments such as "this gizmo is the fulfillment of a dream" or "a pager on steroids" are not uncommon. Why is it so popular? Quite simply, the BlackBerry is a wireless pager that lets you send and receive e-mail without dialing up.

It's one of three product lines from Research in Motion, the others being the RIM Wireless Handheld and the RIM Embedded Radio Modem. The Wireless Handheld is actually the hardware component of the BlackBerry, which is a package deal that includes the handheld, software, and an e-mail account.

Let's go back to awards a sec. And the Oscar goes to... What? Yes, Research in Motion has even won an Academy Award (in 1999), and an Emmy (in 1994). In 1991, before it made wireless devices, RIM created the DigiSync Film KeyKode Reader, a device that reads, decodes, indexes, and retrieves the optical information stored on the edge of motion picture film. It's used around the world in motion picture labs, negative film cutting, and post-production.

Opportunities and Challenges

Research in Motion has strategic alliances—for marketing and for compatibility—with Rogers AT&T Wireless, Bell Mobility, Motient Corporation, BellSouth, EarthLink, BT Cellnet, and Cingular Interactive, as well as working relationships with Sun Microsystems, Nortel, Certicom, IBM, Lucent, and Compaq.

An agreement with Qualcomm in December 2000 licenses RIM to develop devices using Qualcomm's patented CDMA digital wireless technology. This will expand RIM's potential user-base into the huge CDMA cellular and PCS wireless networks.

Most exciting is the introduction in November 2000 of the AOL Mobile Communicator, a branded version of RIM's handheld for AOL's instant messaging and e-mail services.

On the other hand, RIM is facing stiff competition from the Palm Pilot and other wireless devices. This could lead to price cutting and margin erosion.

There has also been concern that a slowing economy has led to inventory buildup of RIM products with its resellers, which may slow sales in the latter half of 2001. For the second quarter to June 2, 2001, revenues rose 184.1 percent and earnings climbed to 5 cents a share from break-even the year before, meeting analyst expectations. Unfortunately, those profits and gains came from investments, not from operations, which ran at a loss.

The stock is extremely volatile and can move significantly in any single trading day. If you buy, pick a good entry point and have a selling plan if the market goes against you.

Financial Highlights

RIM's shares got battered in the tech wreck, falling from $240 in March 2000 to less than $50 in May. The price then climbed back up to $200 in October 2000 before dropping 87.5 percent to $25 in April 2001. The stock started trading between $40 and $60 after that, and likely will stay in that range until operations are in the black.

Research in Motion Ltd. at a Glance

Fiscal Year-end: February

3-Year Return: 90.5%

	1997	1998	1999	2000	2001	6-Year Growth Average (%)	Total (%)
Revenue ($ mlns.)	13.5	33.2	70.5	123.2	339.1	113.9	3,936.9
Net Income ($ mlns.)	0.0	0.5	9.5	15.2	14.3	550.8	1,942.9
Earnings/ Share ($)	–	0.01	0.15	0.22	0.18	–	800.0
Dividend/ Share ($)	–	–	–	–	–	–	–
Price/ Earnings	–	550 - 1020	32.7 - 126.7	47.3 - 1181.8	194.4 - 1333.3	–	–

Table data courtesy of ✓*Canadian Shareowner* **www.shareowner.com**

Stock Growth (Fiscal Year High-Low-Close)

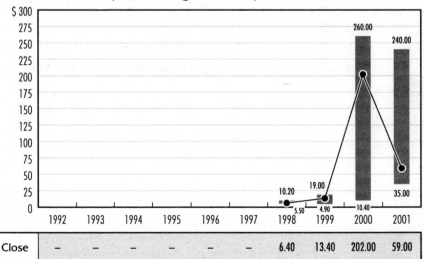

	1992	1993	1994	1995	1996	1997	1998	1999	2000	2001
Close	–	–	–	–	–	–	6.40	13.40	202.00	59.00

WESCAM INC.

649 North Service Road West
Burlington, ON L7P 5B9

Tel: (905) 633-4000   Employees: 500
Fax: (905) 633-4100   Founded: 1974
www.wescam.com   Listed: 1995
Symbol: WSC (TSE)

President and CEO: Mark J. Chamberlain

Share Price Growth	0
Revenue Growth	★ ★ ★ ★ ★
EPS Growth	★ ★ ★
WSC	**8**

About the Company

Who can forget the television images of O.J.'s white Bronco barrelling down a Los Angeles freeway? Or the driver's point-of-view video shot from Indy racecars, or aerial tracking shots of the Nagano Olympics, the America's Cup, or the Tour de France? Or perhaps you've thrilled to the fantastic action shots in films such as *Armageddon*, *Apollo 13*, *GoldenEye*, *Men in Black*, *Mission Impossible*, and *Titanic*?

All were shot using gyro-stabilized cameras supplied by Wescam. This technology was originally developed by the Military Division of Westinghouse Canada for battlefield surveillance. Then in 1974, one of the inventors, Noxon Leavitt, bought the lab equipment and patents and launched Istec Limited. The name was changed to Wescam in October 1994, and a year later the company went public.

Wescam's innovative gyro-cam and wireless technology are now used by the television and motion picture industries, law enforcement agencies, and even aboard the space shuttle. The company both sells and leases equipment and supplies trained camera operators and maintenance technicians. As well as winning 16 Emmys, in 1990 Mr. Leavitt won a special Academy Award for the invention and continued development of the Wescam stabilized camera system.

Wescam revenues have grown 400 percent since going public. Despite market uncertainties, Wescam maintained projections of 5 to 10 percent revenue growth and 20 percent earnings growth for 2001. A poor first quarter was followed by a much improved second quarter, with modest growth in both revenues and earnings. Wescam seems on track for continued growth as the economy improves.

Opportunities and Challenges

Wescam has been active in consolidating its leadership in camera systems for moving platforms through technological development and acquisition. It acquired Creative Resources and Marketing Group in 1994, reorganizing it as Wescam Inc. (USA). Subsequent takeovers included Broadcast Sports Technology, TV2 Limited (in Europe), and most recently, Applied Physics Specialties in March 2001. The company continues to spend about 8 percent of revenues on R&D.

Fiscal 2000 saw Wescam active in over 200 sporting events, including 35 PGA tournaments and 130 car races. Major contracts were landed with the U.S. Navy and the U.S. Coast Guard. Custom products in electronic news gathering were developed for two Los Angeles TV stations. And the company supplied 15 Wescams and 23 camera operators and support crew for the 2000 Summer Olympics in Sydney. Wescam cameras were also used in over 60 motion pictures, including *Jurassic Park III*, *Pearl Harbor*, *Vertical Limit*, and *The Perfect Storm*.

These are recurring and continuing sources of opportunity for Wescam. The market for airborne visual information systems has been estimated at $1.5 billion, and Wescam has ample room for growth in this field alone.

In early 2001, Wescam reorganized the company into two divisions: Commercial Systems and Government Systems. The challenge for Wescam will be to realize operational efficiencies and growth opportunities from these changes.

Financial Highlights

Despite solid growth from 1998 through 2000 in both revenues and earnings, share price increased only modestly. In fact, Wescam did not meet our share price growth standard, actually posting a five-year return of -4.3 percent. The company suffered a loss in 1997, but has seen growing earnings since. And the stock has been on a steady, albeit widely fluctuating, uptrend since it hit a low of $2.25 in August 1997. This growth likely will continue.

Wescam Inc. at a Glance

Fiscal Year-end: October
5-Year Return: -4.3%

	1996	1997	1998	1999	2000	7-Year Growth Average (%)	Total (%)
Revenue ($ mlns.)	64.8	57.6	79.9	123.3	161.0	51.4	875.8
Net Income ($ mlns.)	4.3	-7.0	2.9	4.8	8.2	–	1,266.7
Earnings/ Share ($)	0.35	-0.54	0.20	0.29	0.50	–	400.0
Dividend/ Share ($)	–	–	–	–	–	–	–
Price/ Earnings	15.7 - 22.9	-4.2 - -11.9	14 - 22.5	10.5 - 20.2	7.6 - 15.2	–	–

Table data courtesy of **www.shareowner.com**

Stock Growth (Fiscal Year High-Low-Close)

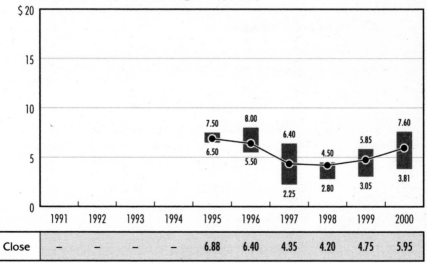

Close	–	–	–	–	6.88	6.40	4.35	4.20	4.75	5.95

BCE INC.

1000 de la Gauchetière Street West, Suite 3700
Montreal, QC H3B 4Y7

Tel: 1-800-339-6353   Employees: 75,000
Fax: (514) 786-3970   Founded: 1880
www.bce.ca   Listed: 1983
Symbol: BCE (TSE) (Also NYSE)

Chairperson and CEO: Jean C. Monty

Share Price Growth		★ ★
Revenue Growth		★
EPS Growth		0
BCE		**3**

About the Company

"Tell me, oh Octopus, I begs, / Is those things arms, or is they legs?"
That bit of doggerel from Ogden Nash could well be applied to BCE.
Or the Stonecutters Song from The Simpsons could be adapted: "Who
puts the glom in conglomerates? We do! We do!"

BCE (Bell Canada Enterprises) is Canada's largest telephone company. Today, it also lays claim to being Canada's leading Internet
company.

Founded in 1880 as the Bell Telephone Company of Canada, it first
became a public company three years later. In 1973, its manufacturing
arm, Northern Electric Manufacturing Limited, was spun off as a public company. Bell retained 90.1 percent of the shares. This spin-off later
became Nortel Networks.

In 1983 Bell Canada Enterprises was created as a parent company for Bell Canada and a holding company for Bell's other interests. The purpose was to separate the regulated telephone company from other non-regulated business interests. Many changes have occurred in the last two years, with the divestiture of most of BCE's Nortel holdings, the launch of the Sympatico Internet service provider, and the acquisition of Lycos, the CTV television network, and the *Globe and Mail*.

BCE owns major interests in three companies involved in Internet connectivity: Bell Canada (80.0 percent), Aliant (45.4 percent), and Bell Expressvu (100 percent). It also owns 70.1 percent of Bell Globemedia, which owns CTV, Sympatico-Lycos, the *Globe and Mail*, and Globe Interactive. Other communications or IT-related holdings include: Teleglobe (96.4 percent), BCE Emergis (66.2 percent), Telsat (100 percent), Excel Communications (95.4 percent), Look Communications (25.3 percent), and CGI Group (43.4 percent).

With interests in connectivity, content, e-commerce, Internet service providers, and IT services, BCE is indeed a titan of the information age. BCE Inc. is the most profitable company in Canada in dollar terms, with profits in 2000 of $4,861 million. That's more than double the profits of runner-up Royal Bank. It is the third-largest company in Canada by market cap after Nortel and Thomson.

Opportunities and Challenges

Recognizing the opportunities offered by the Internet, BCE has jumped in with both feet, managing connectivity and content. It owns the superb Globeinvestor and related websites (a property Thomson should never have let go, in my opinion), as well as CTV, which will provide Internet content when bandwidth improvements make full-motion, full-screen video commonplace. (Yes—we will be watching TV on our computers, and sooner than you might think. Our family hosts a Korean student, and she can already watch Korean TV on the Internet, although the image is small and rather jumpy.)

The full potential of many of BCE's holdings has not yet been realized. BCE has long been held by Canadians as a solid, blue chip stock—a utility—the phone company. It is still that, but it is much more besides. BCE has tremendous upside potential and should be a core long-term holding in everyone's portfolio. BCE was ace stock-picker Patrick McKeough's (of *The Successful Investor* newsletter) choice as the one stock to own for 2001. I'd say it's worth having in 2002 as well.

BCE's biggest challenge is coordinating and integrating the activities of its many tentacles. The market usually does not allot full value to conglomerates, which is why the company divested itself of its rich Nortel holdings. It may have to do the same with other holdings in the future.

Financial Highlights

The financial table for BCE seems out of whack, with revenues dropping almost in half in 2000 from the year before. The share price also took a huge tumble. But this fall was not the tech wreck at work. Rather, BCE divested itself of its substantial interest in Nortel Networks, distributing Nortel shares to its shareholders as a dividend. As a holding company, the company's diverse interests have created a track record that is difficult to interpret. I've tried to calculate the Nortel effect and have given the company the star ratings I derived as a result. Although this stock looks weak by the numbers, it is actually one of the most solid stocks in the book—an unfortunate anomaly.

BCE Inc. at a Glance

Fiscal Year-end: December
10-Year Return: 30.1%

	1996	1997	1998	1999	2000	10-Year Growth Average (%)	10-Year Growth Total (%)
Revenue ($ mlns.)	28,167.0	33,191.0	27,454.0	14,214.0	18,094.0	1.9	-9.0
Net Income ($ mlns.)	958.7	1,221.1	1,925.6	2,384.8	167.5	2.6	-86.4
Earnings/ Share ($)	1.52	1.92	3.02	3.71	0.25	1.9	-87.6
Dividend/ Share ($)	1.36	1.36	1.35	1.37	1.23	-0.4	-3.9
Price/ Earnings	15.5 - 22.7	16 - 25.4	13.2 - 22.5	15.3 - 36.7	123.8 - 800.8	–	–

Table data courtesy of Canadian Shareowner   www.shareowner.com

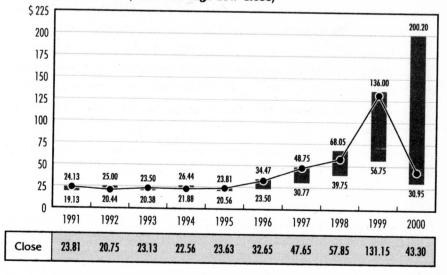

Stock Growth (Fiscal Year High-Low-Close)

| Close | 23.81 | 20.75 | 23.13 | 22.56 | 23.63 | 32.65 | 47.65 | 57.85 | 131.15 | 43.30 |

GLOSSARY

These definitions explain the terms used in the tables and charts accompanying each company profile, and what financial measures the figures represent.

Dividend per Share The cash dividends per share paid to investors during the reporting period. This item has been adjusted to reflect all stock splits and stock dividends.

Earnings per Share (EPS) Calculated by dividing net income by the fully diluted shares outstanding (allowing for the exercise of all warrants and options outstanding). This item has been adjusted to reflect all stock splits and stock dividends.

Fiscal Year-end The last day of this month is the end of the company's 12-month accounting year.

Growth, Average An average year-over-year growth rate.

Growth, Total A simple rate calculated using the starting and ending values only.

Net Income The income, or loss, reported by a company after costs, expenses, and preferred dividends have been subtracted from all revenue for the fiscal year. This data item excludes the effect of all special, discontinued, and extraordinary items.

Price-to-Earnings Ratio (P/E)   Ownership of a share of stock means ownership of one share's worth of a company's earnings per share. A stock's price-to-earnings ratio indicates how much an investor is willing to pay to become the owner of $1.00 of a company's earnings per share.

This ratio is calculated by dividing the company's fiscal year high and low share prices by its earnings per share for the corresponding period. The data are presented as a range starting with the fiscal year low price-to-earnings ratio and ending with the fiscal year high price-to-earnings ratio.

Return   A compound rate reflecting monthly price appreciation (ending May 2001) plus reinvestment of dividends and the compounding effect of dividends paid on reinvested dividends.

Revenue   The dollar amount of annual sales, reduced by discounts and returned merchandise. It is the "top line" figure from which costs are subtracted to determine net income.

Definitions courtesy of ✓*Canadian Shareowner*   **www.shareowner.com**

THE 50 BEST SCIENCE & TECHNOLOGY
STOCKS IN ALPHABETICAL ORDER

Company	Stars	Page
Aastra Technologies Ltd.	15	218
AOL Time Warner Inc.	15	144
ArthroCare Corporation	10	58
ATI Technologies Inc.	9	200
ATS Automation Tooling Systems Inc.	14	102
Axcan Pharma Inc.	11	46
BCE Inc.	3	242
Biovail Corporation	14	38
Bombardier Inc.	12	110
BW Technologies Ltd.	8	122
CAE Inc.	6	130
Calpine Corporation	15	80
Canadian Hydro Developers, Inc.	10	88
Canadian Medical Laboratories Ltd.	6	70
Celestica Inc.	9	204
CGI Group Inc.	15	148
Check Point Software Technologies Ltd.	15	152
C-MAC Industries Inc.	15	222
Cognos Inc.	13	188
Comverse Technology Inc.	15	226
Cree, Inc.	15	98
DuPont Canada Inc.	8	126
EMC Corporation	15	156

Company	Stars	Page
Forest Laboratories, Inc.	11	50
Gennum Corporation	12	114
Intel Corporation	14	184
Internet Security Systems, Inc.	8	208
Magellan Aerospace Corporation	4	138
Magna International Inc.	14	106
MDS Inc.	10	62
Merck & Company	9	66
Mercury Interactive Corporation	15	160
Microsoft Corporation	15	164
Network Appliance, Inc.	15	168
Pason Systems Inc.	11	84
Patheon Inc.	12	42
Pfizer Inc.	11	54
PMC-Sierra, Inc.	15	230
Research in Motion Ltd.	14	234
Sapient Corporation	11	196
Siebel Systems, Inc.	15	172
Silent Witness Enterprises Ltd.	11	118
Solectron Corporation	15	176
Tesma International Inc.	6	134
The Thomson Corporation	4	212
THQ Inc.	13	192
Trican Well Service Ltd.	9	92
Wescam Inc.	8	238
Yahoo! Inc.	15	180
Zenon Environmental Inc.	4	74

INDEX

A

Aastra Technologies Ltd., 15, 218–221
Academic Network for Clinical Research Inc., 71
Academy Award, 235
Alexander, Kobi, 226
Aliant, 243
Allen, Paul, 164
America Online, 144, 145
Andrx Corporation, 40
annual earnings growth, 20
AOL Time Warner Inc., 144–147
Applied Micro Devices, 185
Applied Physics Specialties, 239
Array Technologies Inc., 201
Arthrocare Corporation, 15, 58–61
Association of Professors of Medicine, 71
ATI Technologies Inc., 15, 16, 200–203
ATS Automation Tooling Systems Inc., 102–105
Aventis Pharmaceuticals, 40
Axcan Pharma Inc., 46–49

B

BAE Systems, 131
Bailey, Robert L., 230, 231
Baker, Michael, 56
Bakshi, Rajeev (Rob), 118
Ballard Power, 17
Ballmer, Steven A., 164
Balsillie, Jim, 234
Barrett, Craig R., 184
BCE Emergis, 243

BCE Inc., 15, 242–245
Beaudoin, Laurent, 110
Bell Canada, 243
Bell Canada Enterprises. *See* BCE Inc.
Bell Expressvu, 243
Bell Globemedia, 213, 243
Bell Telephone Company, 242
Belluzzo, Rick, 164
Benedek, Andrew, 74
biology, medicine, and environment
  Arthrocare Corporation, 15, 58–61
  Axcan Pharma Inc., 46–49
  Biovail Corporation, 38–41, 51
  Canadian Medical Laboratories Ltd., 70–73
  Forest Laboratories, Inc., 39, 50–53
  MDS Inc., 62–65
  Merck & Company, Inc., 66–69
  Patheon Inc., 8, 30, 42–45
  Pfizer Inc., 54–57
  sector, 9
  Zenon Environmental Inc., 74–77
Biovail Corporation, 38–41, 51
Blau, 134
Boca Raton Medical Research, 72
Boeing, 140
Bombardier, J.-Armande, 110
Bombardier Inc., 110–113
Boston Scientific, 59
Bourguin-Jallieu, 43
Bristol Aerospace, 139, 140
Bristow, Paul J., 70

Broadcast Sports Technology, 239
Brown, Robert L., 110
Brydon, Bruce D., 38
bull markets, 2–3
Burney, Derek H., 130, 131
Bush, George W., 90
Busicom, 4
business intelligence, 188–191
buy-and-hold philosophy, 23–24
buy right, 19–22
BW Technologies Ltd., 122–125

C
C-MAC Industries Inc., 30, 43,
    222–225
CAE Inc., 15, 130–133
Calpine Corporation, 8–9, 80–83
Canadair, 111
Canadian Explosives Limited, 127
Canadian Hydro Developers, Inc.,
    9, 88–91
Canadian Industries Limited (CIL),
    127
Canadian Medical Laboratories
    Ltd., 70–73
CANSLIM, 20–22
Cardizem, 40
Carson Group, 213
Carswell, 214
Cartwright, Pete, 80
Case, Steve, 144
Celestica Inc., 17, 30, 43, 204–207
CGI Group Inc., 8, 30, 148–151, 243
Chamberlain, Mark J., 238
Charles Scribner's Sons, 214
Check Point Software Technologies
    Ltd., 152–155
Cipher Pharmaceuticals, 71
Cisco, 16
Cobbe, Murray, 92
Coblation process, 59
Cognos Inc., 17, 30, 188–191
Colcleugh, David W., 126
Compaq Computer, 6

Comverse Infosys, 226
Comverse Network Systems,
    226–227
Comverse Technology Inc., 16,
    226–229
contract manufacturing, 177–178
convergence, 29
Cosma, 107
Creative Resources and Marketing
    Group, 239
Cree, Inc., 98–101
criteria, 12–13
CTV, 243
current quarterly earnings growth,
    20
customer relations management
    software (CRM), 172–175
CyberBranch, 149
CyberMedix Inc., 70
Cygnal Technologies, 16

D
DaimlerChrysler, 6
Decoma, 107, 108
Deloitte & Touche Fast 500/50
    lists, 10–11, 59, 172, 218
Dialog, 213
diversification, 18–19
dividend per share, 246
DJ Pharma, 39
Dow Jones Industrial Average, 23
du Pont, Lammot, 126
Duke Energy, 81
DuPont Canada Inc., 126–129

E
earnings per share (EPS), 246
Ebay, 27
Edwards, N. Murray, 138
Egan, Richard J., 156, 157
E.I. du Pont de Nemours, 127
electronic games, 192–195
electronics manufacturing services
    (EMS), 176–179

Embraer SA, 111–112
EMC Corporation, 156–159, 168, 170
Emmy, 235
Encal Energy, 82
energy
    Calpine Corporation, 8–9, 80–83
    Canadian Hydro Developers, Inc., 9, 88–91
    growth industry, 30
    Pason Systems Inc., 84–87, 94
    sector, 9
    Trican Well Services Ltd., 6–7, 30, 92–95
environment. *See* biology, medicine, and environment
Eralmetall, 134
Erhart, Charles, 54
Ethicon, 59
Excel Communications, 243

F
Fairchild Semiconductor, 185
Falk, Herbert, 46
Farrell, Brian J., 192
Filo, David, 180
fiscal year-end, 246
Fleet Aerospace, 138
Fleet Industries, 139
Forest Laboratories, Inc., 39, 50–53
Forestry Systems, 131
Fort Frances Inc., 70

G
Galephar Pharmaceutical Research, 71
Gates, William H., 164, 165, 166
General Electric, 164
General Motors, 145
general online resources, 32
Genesis Microchip, 16
Gennum Corporation, 114–117
Gilmartin, Raymond V., 66
Gingl, Manfred, 134

Global ADSI Solutions, 219
Globeinvestor, 243
Godin, Serge, 148
Goodman, Kenneth E., 50
Gosselin, Leon, 46, 47
Greenberg, Jerry A., 196
Greenhaven Books, 213
Grove, Andrew S., 184
growth, average, 246
growth, total, 246
Gyyr, 119

H
H. Lundbeck, 50
HAC Corporation, 135
Hamilton Powder Company, 126
Harrington, Richard J., 212
Hartford Research Group, 72
Hill, Jim, 84, 85
Ho, K.Y., 200–201
Hoechst Marion Roussel, 43
Hoffman-LacRoche, 43
Honeywell, 223
Hunter, F. Neal, 98

I
IBM, 4, 168, 204, 205
Imbeau, André, 148
IMRglobal, 149
industry
    ATS Automation Tooling Systems Inc., 102–105
    Bombardier Inc., 110–113
    BW Technologies Ltd., 122–125
    CAE Inc., 15, 130–133
    Cree, Inc., 98–101
    DuPont Canada Inc., 126–129
    Gennum Corporation, 114–117
    Magellan Aerospace Corporation, 15, 138–141
    Magna International Inc., 30, 106–109, 223
    sector, 9
    Silent Witness Enterprises Ltd.,

30, 118–121
Tesma International Inc., 30, 107,
    108, 134–137
information technology
    AOL Time Warner Inc., 144–147
    ATI Technologies Inc., 15, 16,
        200–203
    Celestica Inc., 17, 30, 43,
        204–207
    CGI Group Inc., 8, 30, 148–151,
        243
    Check Point Software
        Technologies Ltd., 152–155
    Cognos Inc., 17, 30, 188–191
    EMC Corporation, 156–159,
        168, 170
    Intel Corporation, 4, 184–187
    Internet Security Systems, Inc.,
        15, 208–211
    Mercury Interactive
        Corporation, 16, 30, 160–163
    Microsoft Corporation, 6, 145,
        164–167
    Network Appliance, Inc.,
        157–158, 168–171
    Sapient Corporation, 196–199
    sector, 9
    Siebel Systems, Inc., 30, 172–175
    Solectron Corporation, 176–179,
        224
    Thomson Corporation, 212–215
    THQ Inc., 15, 192–195
    Yahoo! Inc., 180–183
innovation, 4–5
institutional sponsorship, 22
Intel Corporation, 4, 184–187
the Internet, 30
Internet research, 31–33
Internet Security Systems, Inc., 15,
    208–211
Intier, 108
Invotronics, 223
IOB, 213
Istec Limited, 238

J
J.-Armande Bombardier Museum,
    111
Janna Systems, 12, 173
Johnson & Johnson, 59
Jouveinal Inc., 47
Juniper Networks, 16, 206

K
Kachina Award, 231
Kavlico Corporation, 223
Keating, J. Ross, 88
Keating, John D., 88
KEFI Exchange, 89–90
King, Stephen, 161
Klaus, Christopher W., 208–209
Kyoto Accord, 90

L
La Ley, 213
LabCare Inc., 70
Landan, Amnon, 160
Langley Aerospace, 139, 140
Laurentian Bank, 29–30, 149
Lazaridis, Mike, 234
leadership, 21–22
Leavitt, Noxon, 238, 239
Levin, Gerald, 144
Lewitt, Wilfred G., 62
Lizotte-MacPherson, Linda, 197
Lohnerwerke Gmbh, 111
Look Communications, 243
Lucent Press, 213
Lucent Technologies, 29, 206

M
Macmillan, 214
MaGee, J. Marvin, 204
Magellan Aerospace Corporation,
    15, 138–141
Magna Entertainment, 108
Magna International Inc., 30,
    106–109, 223
Magna Mirrors, 107

Magna Steyr Group, 107, 108, 135
Malcolm Baldrige National Quality
    Award, 176–177
Mallett, Jeffrey, 180
Maple Group, 134
Marino, Roger, 157
market direction, 22
Matthews, Bill, 126
Mayo Clinic, 46
McKinnell, Henry A., 54
McWalter, Ian L., 114
MDS Inc., 62–65
medical breakthroughs, 30–31
medicine. *See* biology, medicine,
    and environment
Melnyk, Eugene N., 38
Mendoza, Thomas F., 168
Merck & Company, Inc., 66–69
Merck Frosst Canada, 66
Merck-Medco Managed Care, 67
Mercury Interactive Corporation,
    16, 30, 160–163
Microsoft Corporation, 6, 145,
    164–167
Mims, David W., 46, 47
Monty, Jean C., 242
Moore, Gordon, 185
Moore, J. Stuart, 196
Mull, John D., 70

N
Nacht, Marius, 152, 153
nanotechnology, 30
natural gas. *See* energy
Neill, Richard A., 138
Nelson, 214
net income, 246
Network Appliance, Inc., 157–158,
    168–171
Network Appliance Canada,
    169–170
news, 20–21
Nichia Corporation, 100
Nicol, James, 106

Nishimura, Koichi, 176, 177
Nitres Corporation, 99
Noonan, Thomas E., 208, 209
Nortel Networks, 15–16, 29, 219,
    223, 242, 243, 244
Northern Electric Manufacturing
    Limited, 242
Novoquest Research, 71
Noyce, Robert, 185
nVidia, 16

O
oil industry. *See* energy
Oilfield Stimulation Services, 94
Onex Corporation, 204
online newsletters, 33
online resources, 31
online stock lists, 33
Oracle, 16, 173–174
Orenda Aerospace, 139
Orton, Dave, 200
outsourcing, 29–30

P
Pacific Gas and Electric, 82
PAID Prescriptions, 67
Pason Systems Inc., 84–87, 94
Patheon Inc., 8, 30, 42–45
Pechiney Group, 149
PeopleSoft, 174
Pfizer, Charles, 54
Pfizer Inc., 54–57
Pharma Medica Research, 71
Phoenix International Life
    Sciences, 63, 64
PMC-Sierra, Inc., 230–233
Polistuk, Eugene V., 204
price/earnings ratio, 26–29, 247
Primark, 213
Prometric, 213
Prozac, 52

Q
QLT Phototherapeutics, 47

Qualcomm, 235

R
Research in Motion Ltd., 17, 30, 234–237
return, 247
revenue, 247
Rogers, John A., 62
Ruettgers, Michael C., 156

S
SAP, 174
Sapient Corporation, 196–199
Saturn Development Group, 231
Scandipharm, 47
Schwartz, Gerald, 204
Schwed, Gil, 152, 153
science and technology stocks, defined, 5–9
sell right, 22–25
selling plan, 12, 23–25
Semel, Terry, 180, 181, 182
Shen, Anthony, 218
Shen, Francis, 218
Short Brothers PLC, 111
Siebel, Thomas M., 172, 173
Siebel Systems, Inc., 12, 30, 172–175
Siemens, 193
Sierra Semiconductor, 231
Sierra Wireless, 16
Silent Witness Enterprises Ltd., 30, 118–121
Slater, Cody Z., 122
Solectron Corporation, 176–179, 224
Solomon, Howard, 50
Stanley Works, 119–120
Steyr-Daimler-Puch, 107
stock chart channels, 25–26
Stronach, Belinda, 106, 108
Stronach, Frank, 106, 107
Summit Research, 72
Sun Microsystems, 16, 205

Superior Cementers, 93
supply and demand, 21
Sweet & Maxwell, 214
Swoboda, Charles M., 98

T
Tapp, L.G., 102
Tedford, Robert C., 42
telecommunications
    Aastra Technologies Ltd., 15, 218–221
    BCE Inc., 15, 242–245
    C-MAC Industries Inc., 30, 43, 222–225
    Comverse Technology Inc., 16, 226–229
    PMC-Sierra, Inc., 230–233
    Research in Motion Ltd., 17, 30, 234–237
    sector, 9
    Wescam Inc., 30, 238–241
Teleglobe, 243
Telsat, 243
Tesma International Inc., 30, 107, 108, 134–137
Teve Pharmaceuticals, 39
Thomson, David, 214
Thomson, Kenneth R., 212, 213, 214
Thomson, Roy, 212–213
Thomson & Thomson, 214
Thomson Corporation, 212–215
Thomson/Frist Call, 214
Thomson Newspapers Limited, 213
THQ Inc., 15, 192–195
Time Warner, 144, 146
Time Warner Cable, 145
Trican Well Services Ltd., 6–7, 30, 92–95
Tucci, Joseph M., 156
Turner Broadcasting, 145
TV2 Limited, 239
Tyco Electronics, 115

U

Ulticom, 226
Ungerman, Jerry, 152
Upjohn Canada, 43

V

Vantive, 174
Viagra, 56
voice mail, 226–229
volatility, 22

W

Wadsworth, 214
Warmenhoven, Dan, 168, 169
Warner Lambert, 55, 56
Wave Technologies, 213
Wescam Inc., 30, 238–241
Wescam Inc. (USA), 239

Westinghouse Canada, 238
Westlaw, 214
Wilson, Lynton R., 130
wireless technology, 30, 193,
    234–237
Woerner, Klaus D., 102, 103
Wood, Dennis, 222
World Trade Organization, 112
Wyeth-Ayerst, 47

Y

Yahoo! Inc., 180–183
Yang, Jerry, 180

Z

Zambonini, Renato, 188, 190
Zenon Environmental Inc., 74–77
Zenon Technologies, 15

Notes

Notes

Notes

the 50 BEST for **CANADIANS**
series

The 50 Best Stocks for Canadians

Lori Bamber and Gene Walden
ISBN 0-55335-012-X

Every portfolio needs a core of blue-chip stocks.
Build your portfolio with these 50 proven low-risk,
long-term winners, and prosper over the long haul.

The 50 Best Small Cap Stocks for Canadians

Lori Bamber and Gene Walden
ISBN 0-55335-013-8

Small cap stocks offer greater risks and also greater rewards. Add small cap stocks to your portfolio, and cash
in on those rewards!

The 50 Best Science & Technology Stocks for Canadians

Marco den Ouden
ISBN 0-55335-015-4

Take advantage of the power of innovation and invest
in science and technology companies on the cutting
edge of development. Science and technology stocks
offer some of the best opportunities for investors in the
marketplace.